Collins

Maths EXPERT 1

Author | Prabha Sethy

Preface

Collins Maths Expert is a series of eight books for Classes 1 to 8. The series adheres to the guidelines of the **National Education Policy (NEP) 2020** and aligns with the vision of the ***National Initiative for Proficiency in Reading with Understanding and Numeracy*** **(NIPUN Bharat)**.

In this series, the approach is **"Less Is More"** and **"Drill and Practice"**. It provides all the basic information considered essential in attaining the objectives of mathematics education. All concept explanations are *simple* and *concise* with more *focus on Solved Examples*. The content has also been organized in a horizontal and vertical progression. The language used is child friendly and age appropriate.

This series aims to provide adequate opportunities to help students develop problem solving and critical thinking skills through solved examples, practice questions, formulas, tables, images and illustrations. Most of the solved examples are constructed from daily life situations requiring the student to apply mathematical principles and formula for their solution. Varieties of questions have been included to cater to all level of students. Sufficient provision for practice, revision and review have been provided through adequate number of questions. While citing examples from real life, an effort has been made to make the content inclusive with respect to race, gender, regions, religion, food, flora, fauna, festivals, etc.

We would like to take this opportunity to thank all the teachers who reviewed the books and provided their invaluable feedback, which helped in improving the quality of the content. Any suggestions or constructive criticism from the users are welcome. We shall try to incorporate those in the future editions.

Authors

About the Features

The key features of ***Collins Maths Expert*** series are completely aligned with National Education Policy (NEP) 2020.

Let's Recap!: A variety of questions based on the previous grade for quick recapitulation

Prior Knowledge: List of topics to help construct connections between old and new knowledge

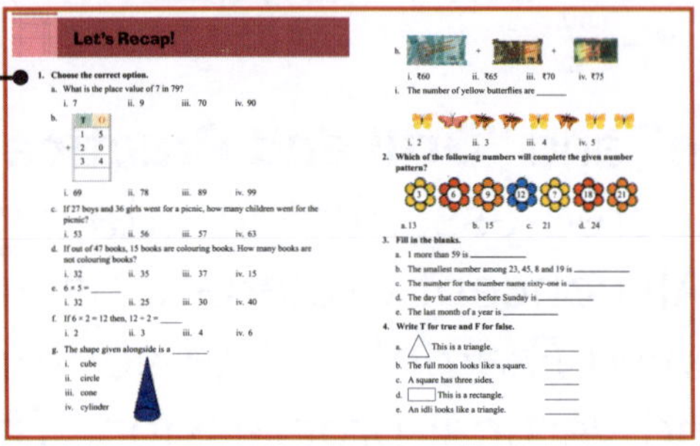

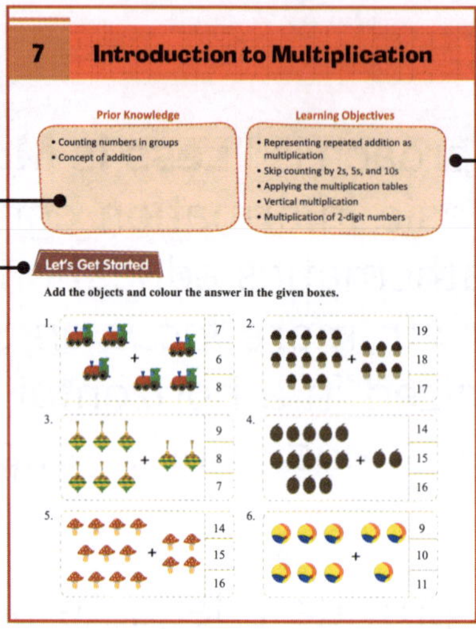

Learning Objectives: List of main topics that will be covered in a chapter

Let's Get Started: Interactive exercise to begin a chapter with real-life connect and addressing 21st Century Skills

Solved Examples: A variety of worked out examples based on each topic

Alert: Snippets to clear common misconceptions and mistakes

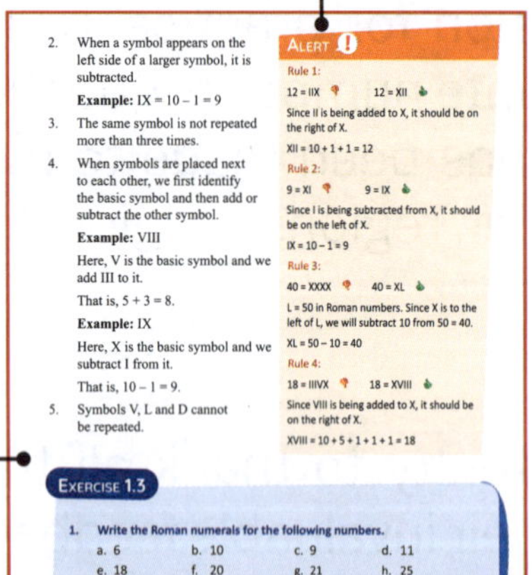

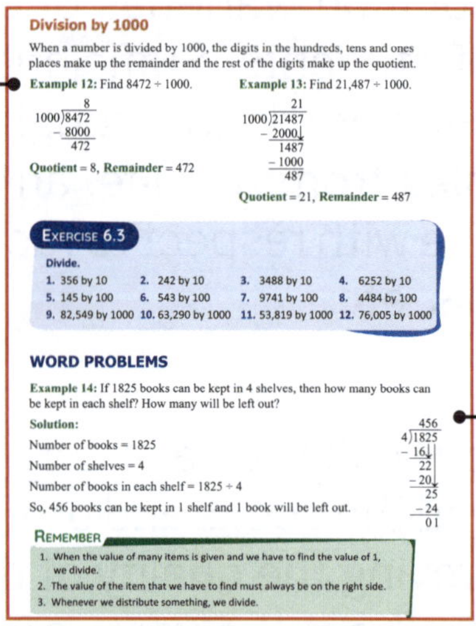

Exercise: Purposefully designed in-text exercises

Remember: Important points for quick reference

Word Problems:

Textual questions based on real-life situations

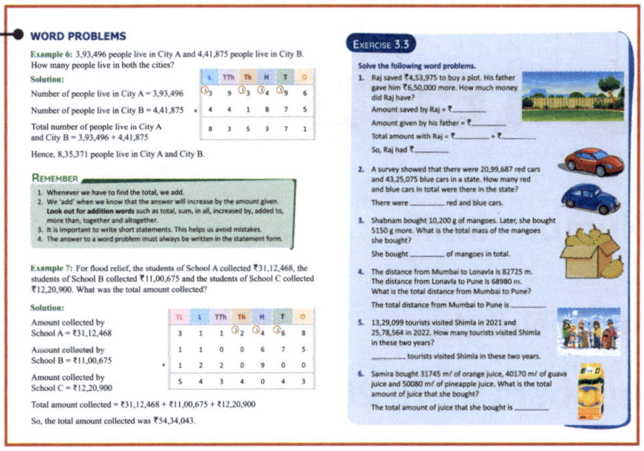

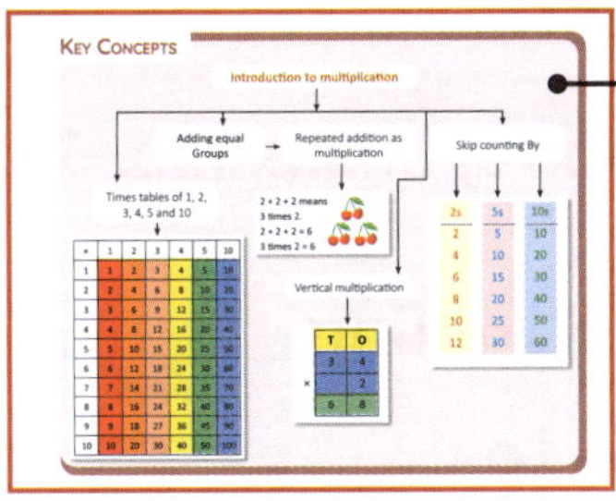

Key Concepts:

A graphic organizer to recap the chapter

Revision Exercise:

Variety of questions based on the topics covered in the chapter

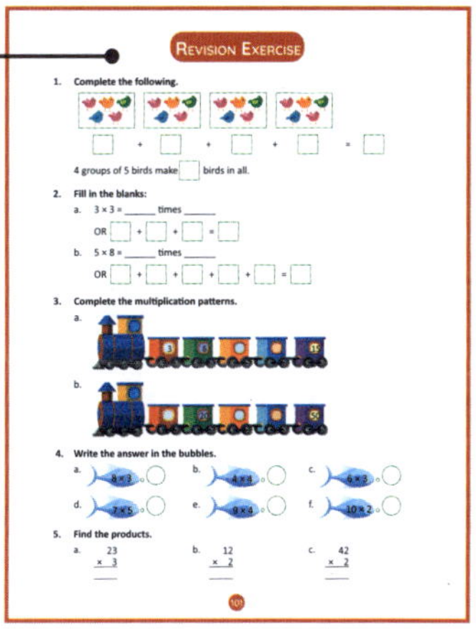

Test Paper:

Variety of questions based on the entire book

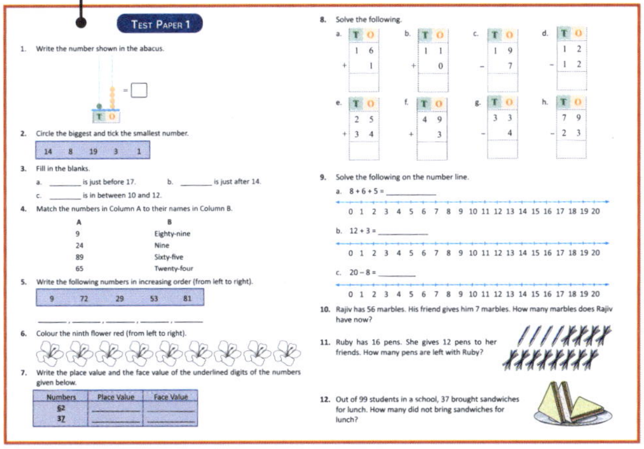

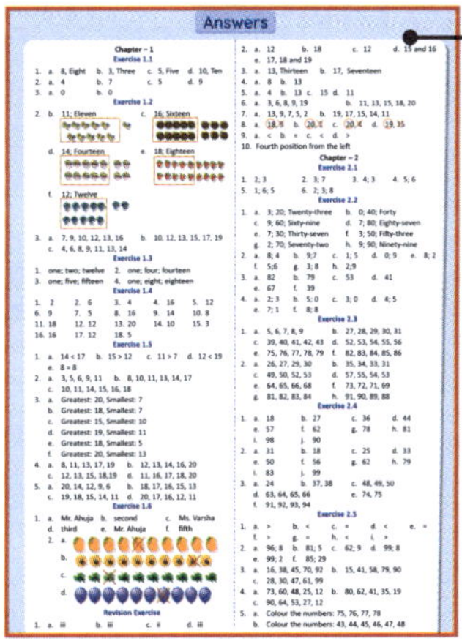

Answer Keys:

Solution to Exercises and Revision Exercise

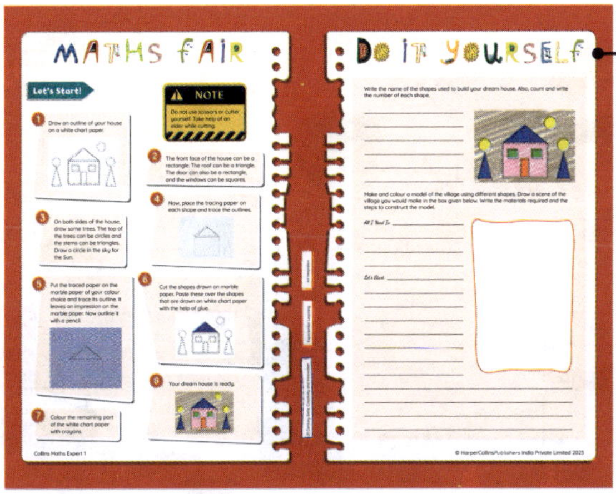

Poster:

Hands-on/STEAM-based activities to develop 21st Century Skills

Contents

Pre-Number Skills

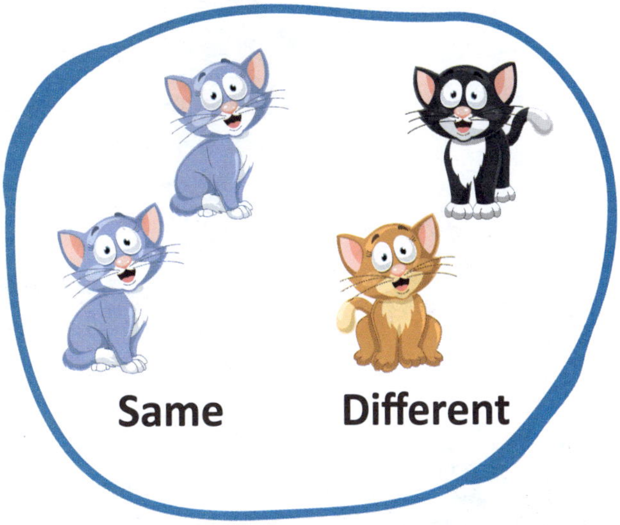

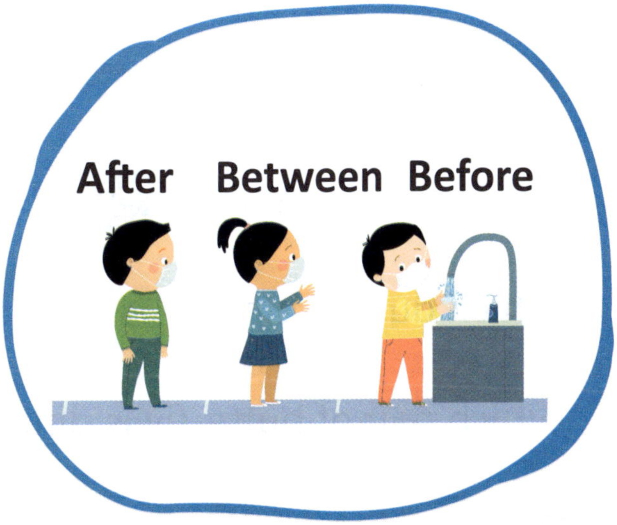

Worksheet

Use the above picture to solve. Circle the answer.

1. Which bird comes after the  ?  

2. Which duck is near the  ?  

3. Which tree is thick?  

4. What is far from the  ?  

5. Which duck is big?  

6. Which pair of butterfly is different?  

7. Which tree has more fruits?  

1 Numbers up to 20

Prior Knowledge

- Pre-number concepts
- Same and different
- Before, after and between

Learning Objectives

- Numerals 1 to 20 and their number names
- Use the words 'before', 'after' and 'between'
- Introduction to zero
- Representation of numbers on an abacus
- Comparing and ordering numbers up to 20
- Ordinal numbers

Let's Get Started

Complete the table.

	Numeral	Number Name
	1	One
		Two
	3	Three
	4	
		Five

	7	
		Eight

INTRODUCTION TO ZERO

When we take away 1 apple from 3 apples, we get 2 apples.

Now take away 1 more apple, we are left with only 1 apple.

Now take away one more apple, we are left with no apples.

When we are left with no quantity of an object, we say that there is zero number of that object. We write **zero** as '0'.

Numeral	Number Name
0	Zero

Example 1: How many honey bees are left?

□ honey bees

1 → honey bee flies away

→

Solution: There are 0 honey bees on the flower.

Example 2: How many coloured pencils are left?

□ coloured pencils

8 → coloured pencils are taken away

→

Solution: There are 0 coloured pencils in the pencil holder.

> **REMEMBER**
> - The numbers 0 to 9 have only one digit.
> - The number 10 is the first and the smallest 2-digit number.

THE NUMBER 10

 and  make 

9 balls | 1 ball | a bunch of 10 balls

Now we know that 9 and 1 more make ten.
We write **ten** as '10'.

Numeral	Number Name
10	Ten

Exercise 1.1

1. Count and write the numerals and their names.

		Numeral	Number Name
a.			
b.			
c.			
d.			

2. Count the number of objects and circle the correct number. One has been done for you.

a. 

3	4	5

b. 

7	8	9

c. 

4	6	5

d. 

6	8	9

3. Fill in the blanks.

a. I take away 4 cookies from 4 cookies, I will be left with ____________ cookies.

b. After taking away 6 sharpeners from 6 sharpeners, ____________ sharpeners will be left.

NUMBERS FROM 11 TO 20

Let's count the numbers from 11 to 20.

10 crayons and 1 crayon make eleven. **11**

10 flowers and 2 flowers make twelve. **12**

10 parachutes and 3 parachutes make thirteen. **13**

10 ducks and 4 ducks make fourteen. **14**

10 rings and 5 rings make fifteen. **15**

10 umbrellas and 6 umbrellas make sixteen. **16**

10 toy cars and 7 toy cars make seventeen. **17**

10 pears and 8 pears make eighteen. **18**

10 ice cream cones and 9 ice cream cones make nineteen. **19**

10 spoons and 10 spoons make twenty. **20**

EXERCISE 1.2

1. **Trace the numeral and number name.**

11	E L E V E N
11	ELEVEN
12	T W E L V E
12	TWELVE
13	T H I R T E E N
13	THIRTEEN
14	F O U R T E E N
14	FOURTEEN
15	F I F T E E N
15	FIFTEEN
16	S I X T E E N
16	SIXTEEN
17	S E V E N T E E N
17	SEVENTEEN
18	E I G H T E E N
18	EIGHTEEN
19	N I N E T E E N
19	NINETEEN
20	T W E N T Y
20	TWENTY

2. Circle the objects to make groups of tens. Then count the objects. Write the numerals and their names. One has been done for you.

a. 

15 ______ Fifteen ______

b. 

______ ______

c. 

______ ______

d. 

______ ______

e. 

______ ______

f. 

______ ______

3. Fill in the missing numbers.

a.

6	
8	
11	
14	
15	

b.

9	
11	
14	
	16
18	

c.

	5
7	
10	
12	

NUMBERS ON AN ABACUS

We use an abacus for counting numbers. An abacus has 2 rods for putting beads. The left rod represents Tens (T) and the right rod represents Ones (O).

There is 1 bead in the tens rod and 2 beads in the ones rod. So, the number shown on the abacus is 12.

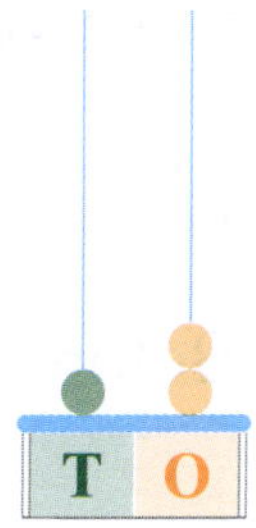

REMEMBER

No bead in the ones rod represents the value 0.

Example 3: Represent the number 19 on an abacus.

Solution: Draw 1 bead in the tens rod and 9 beads in the ones rod.

So, 1 ten and 9 ones make 19.

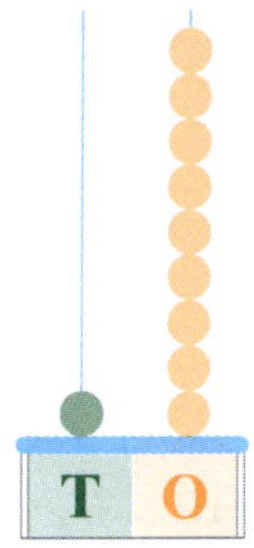

EXERCISE 1.3

Count the beads shown on the abacus and fill in the blanks.

1.

_______ ten and _______ ones make _______

2.

_______ ten and _______ ones make _______

3.

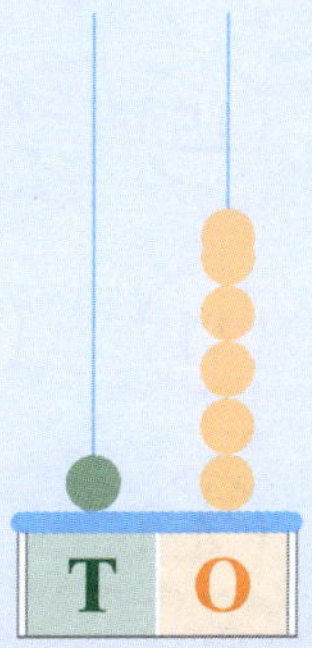

_______ ten and _______ ones make _______

4.

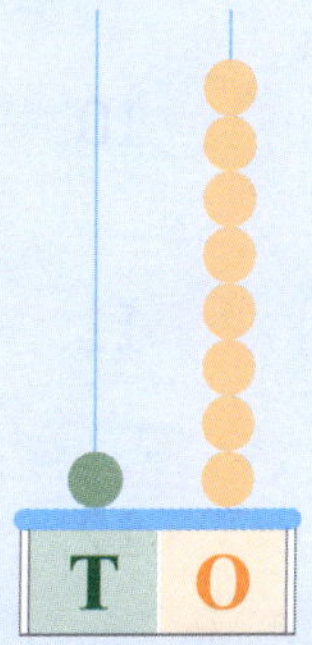

_______ ten and _______ ones make _______

BEFORE, AFTER AND IN BETWEEN

Look at the number strip given below.

0	1	2	3	4	5	6	7	8	9	10	11	12	13	14	15	16	17	18	19	20

Before ← 9 | 10 → Between | 11 → After

1 is just before 2.

2 is just before 3.

6, 11 and 14 are before 18.

15 is in between 14 and 16.

14, 15 and 16 are between 13 and 17.

3 is just after 2.

2 is just after 1.

13, 16 and 19 are after 10.

17 and 18 are between 16 and 19.

16, 17, 18 and 19 are between 15 and 20.

EXERCISE 1.4

What comes just before? What comes in between? What comes just after?

	Before			In Between			After
1.	◯ 3	7.	4 ◯ 6	13.	19 ◯
2.	◯ 7	8.	15 ◯ 17	14.	9 ◯
3.	◯ 5	9.	13 ◯ 15	15.	2 ◯
4.	◯ 17	10.	7 ◯ 9	16.	15 ◯
5.	◯ 13	11.	17 ◯ 19	17.	11 ◯
6.	◯ 10	12.	11 ◯ 13	18.	4 ◯

COMPARISON OF NUMBERS

Greater Than

Count the number of blueberries in both bunches.

8 blueberries

3 blueberries

8 is **greater than** 3.

‘>’ is the symbol of ‘greater than’.

We write as $8 > 3$.

Smaller Than

Count the number of balloons in both bunches.

7 balloons

11 balloons

7 is **smaller than** 11.

‘<’ is the symbol of ‘smaller than’.

We write as $7 < 11$.

Equal To

2 gift boxes

2 party caps

2 is **equal to** 2.

‘=’ is the symbol of ‘equal to’.

We write as $2 = 2$.

REMEMBER

- When two numbers have the same value, we say they are equal.

Comparison of Numbers Using a Number Line

A **number line** helps us to understand numbers. It has numbers placed on it at equal distance.

Look at the following number line that shows numbers from 0 to 10.

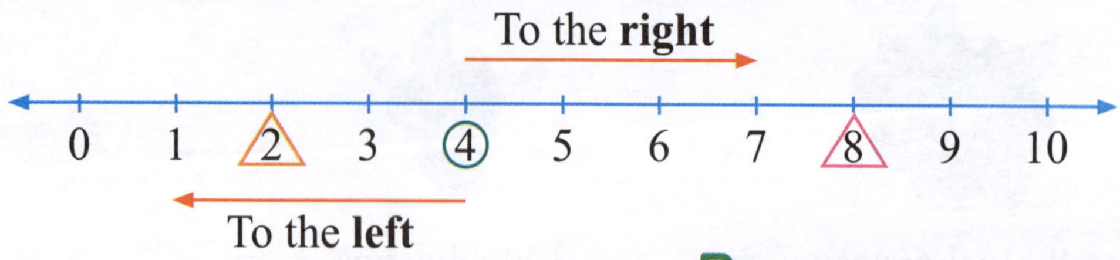

Here, 2 comes before 4. 2 is smaller than 4.

So 2 < 4.

Next, 8 comes after 4. 8 is greater than 4.

So 8 > 4.

> **REMEMBER**
> - The number to the left of a given number is smaller than the given number.
> - The number to the right of a given number is greater than the given number.

Example 4: Fill in the gaps on the number line given below.

0 1 2 __ 4 __ __ 7 __ 9 __

Solution:

0 1 2 3 4 5 6 7 8 9 10

Example 5: Fill in the gaps on the number line starting from 9.

9 10 __ 12 13 14 __ __ __ 18 19 20

Solution:

9 10 11 12 13 14 15 16 17 18 19 20

ORDERING NUMBERS

Increasing order or ascending order of numbers is the order in which the numbers are written from the smallest to the greatest.

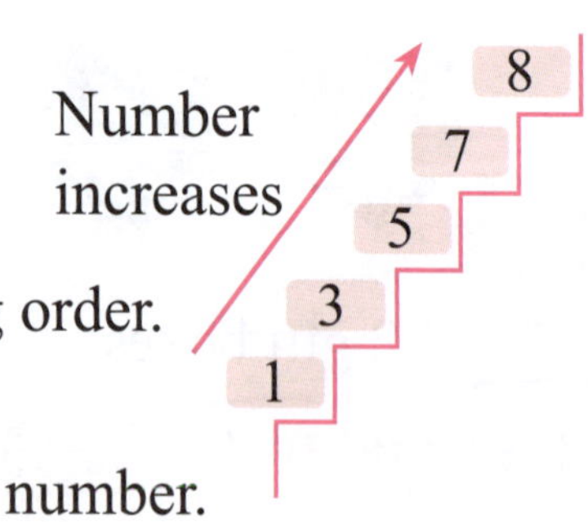

Example 6: Write the following numbers in the increasing order.

a. 8, 3, 6, 1, 2 b. 14, 11, 19, 18, 13

Solution: a. 8 is the greatest number and 1 is the smallest number.

Since 1 < 2 < 3 < 6 < 8

The numbers in the increasing order are 1, 2, 3, 6, 8.

b. 19 is the greatest number and 11 is the smallest number.

Since $11 < 13 < 14 < 18 < 19$

The numbers in the increasing order are 11, 13, 14, 18, 19.

Decreasing order or descending order of numbers is the order in which the numbers are written from the greatest to the smallest.

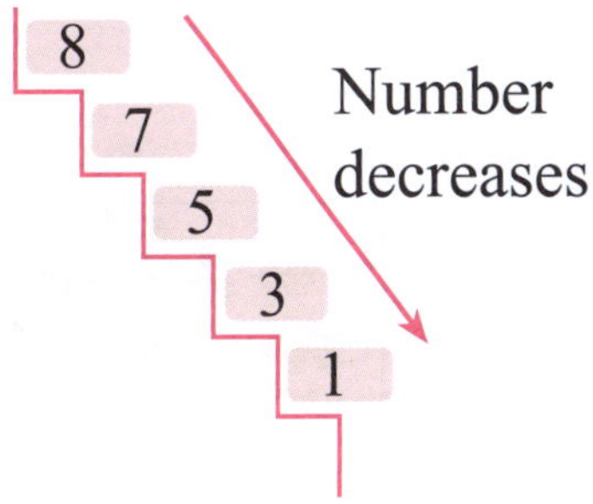

Example 7: Write the following numbers in the decreasing order.

a. 5, 8, 7, 2, 4 b. 14, 17, 6, 19, 10

Solution: a. 8 is the greatest number and 2 is the smallest number.

Since, $8 > 7 > 5 > 4 > 2$

The numbers in the decreasing order are 8, 7, 5, 4, 2.

b. 19 is the greatest number and 6 is the smallest number.

Since $19 > 17 > 14 > 10 > 6$

The numbers in the decreasing order are 19, 17, 14, 10, 6.

EXERCISE 1.5

1. Count and compare using >, < or = signs. One has been done for you.

a.

14 (<) 17

b.

☐ ◯ ☐

c.

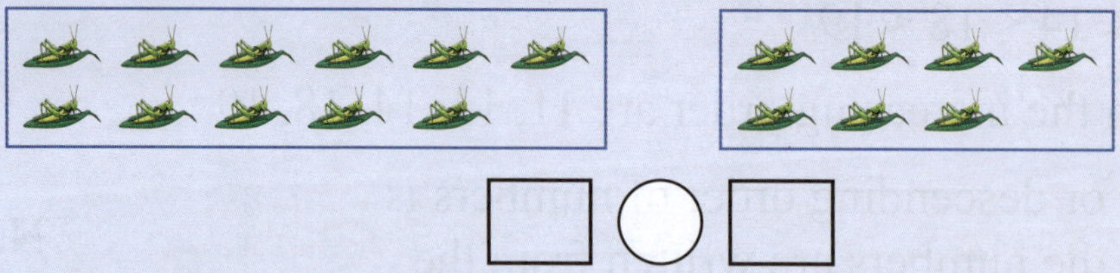

d.

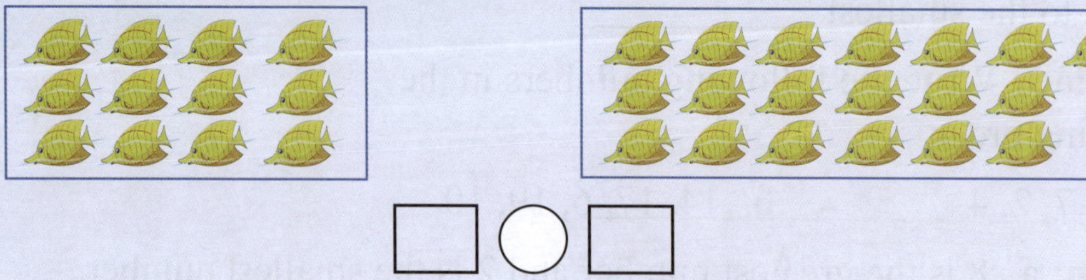

e.

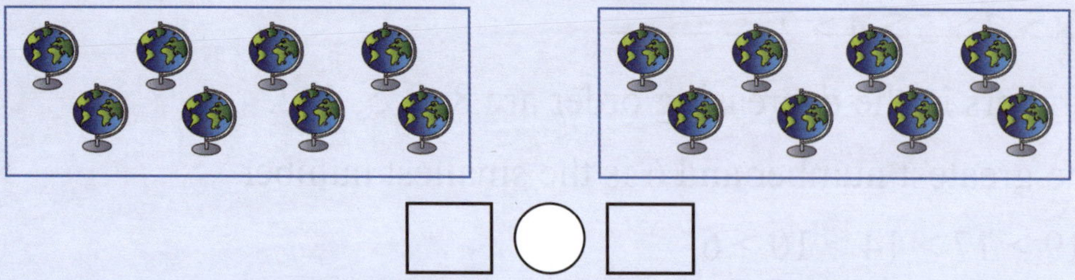

2. Fill in the gaps on the number lines given below.

a. 2 __ 4 __ __ 7 8 __ 10 __ 12

b. 7 __ 9 __ __ 12 __ __ 15 16 __

c. __ __ 12 13 __ __ __ 17 __ 19 20

3. For each of the following, circle the greatest number and cross out the smallest number.

a. 19 11 7 20 8

b. 15 11 18 7 13

c. 12 15 13 10 11

d. 17 11 13 19 15

e. 9 12 5 18 16

f. 20 14 13 18 17

4. **Write the following numbers in the increasing order.**

a. 13, 19, 8, 11, 17 ______________________

b. 20, 14, 12, 16, 13 ______________________

c. 15, 19, 13, 18, 12 ______________________

d. 18, 11, 17, 20, 16 ______________________

5. **Write the following numbers in the decreasing order.**

a. 14, 9, 12, 6, 20 ______________________

b. 17, 15, 16, 13, 18 ______________________

c. 11, 18, 19, 15, 14 ______________________

d. 12, 17, 20, 16, 11 ______________________

ORDINAL NUMBERS

Look at the following table.

Position	1	2	3	4	5	6	7	8	9	10
Ordinal	First	Second	Third	Fourth	Fifth	Sixth	Seventh	Eighth	Ninth	Tenth
Written as	1st	2nd	3rd	4th	5th	6th	7th	8th	9th	10th

The numbers such as **first**, **second**, **third** and **fourth** tell us the position of an object. These numbers are called **ordinal numbers.**

Look at the pictures. Starting from the left, fill in the blanks with the correct ordinals. One has been done for you.

Left

The ___first___ picture is an .

The __________ picture is a .

The __________ picture is a .

The __________ picture is a 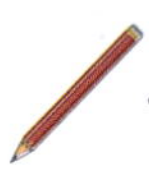.

The __________ picture is a .

The __________ picture is a .

The __________ picture is a .

The __________ picture is a .

The __________ picture is an .

The __________ picture is a .

Exercise 1.6

1. The picture is of a building with 6 floors. Answer the following questions. Note that Mr Gupta lives on the first floor.

a. Who lives on the fourth floor? ______________

b. Ms Shyama lives on the ______________ floor.

c. Who lives on the sixth floor? ______________

d. Mr Khan lives on the ______________ floor.

e. ______________ lives between the third floor and the fifth floor.

f. Mr John lives on the ______________ floor.

2. Cross (×) the picture as directed moving from left to right.

a. 5th mango 

b. 9th flower 

c. 3rd leaf 

d. 7th balloon 

Key Concepts

Numbers up to 20

Count, read and write

0	zero			
1	one		11	eleven
2	two		12	twelve
3	three		13	thirteen
4	four		14	fourteen
5	five		15	fifteen
6	six		16	sixteen
7	seven		17	seventeen
8	eight		18	eighteen
9	nine		19	nineteen
10	ten		20	twenty

Representation on abacus

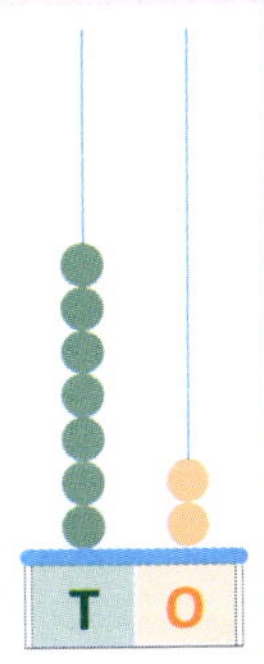

Before, after and between

13, 14, 15

13 is before 14.

15 is after 14.

14 is between 13 and 15.

Compare and order

8 6 20 12

Smallest to greatest:

$6 < 8 < 12 < 20$

It is in ascending order.

Greatest to smallest:

$20 > 12 > 8 > 6$

It is in descending order.

Ordinal Numbers

1st	first
2nd	second
3rd	third
4th	fourth
5th	fifth
6th	sixth
7th	seventh
8th	eighth
9th	ninth
10th	tenth

Revision Exercise

1. Choose the correct option.

a. Which is the greatest number?

i. 4 ii. 2 iii. 7 iv. 5

b. The number 6 is written as ________.

i. five ii. four iii. six iv. two

c. Which is the smallest number?

i. 1 ii. 0 iii. 6 iv. 9

d. Which group shows 7 balloons?

i. 

ii. 

iii. 

iv. 

2. Fill in the blanks.

a. ________ is just before 13.

b. ________ is just after 17.

c. ________ is in between 11 and 13.

d. ________ and ________ are between 14 and 17.

e. ________, ________ and ________ are between 16 and 20.

3. Write the numbers and the number names of the following.

a. 

Number ________ Number name ______________________

b. 

Number ________ Number name ______________________

4. Count the number of pictures and circle the correct number for each of the following.

a. 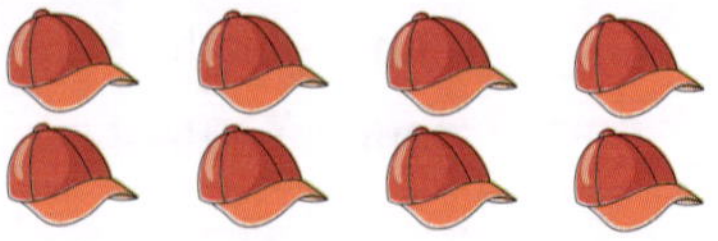

10	8	6

b. 

14	17	13

5. Count the beads shown on the abacus and write the numbers.

a. 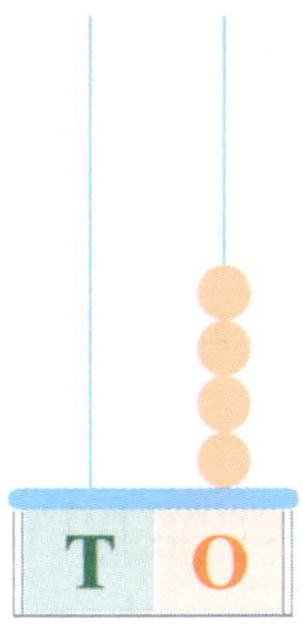

____

b. 

____

c. 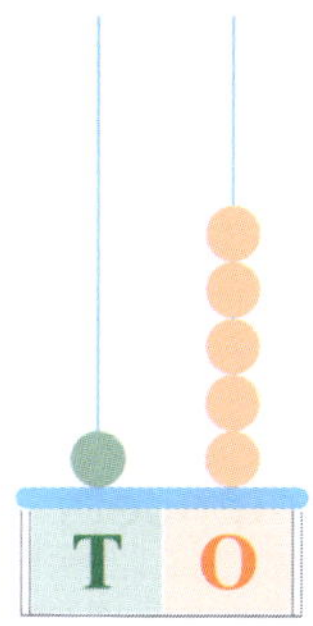

____

d. 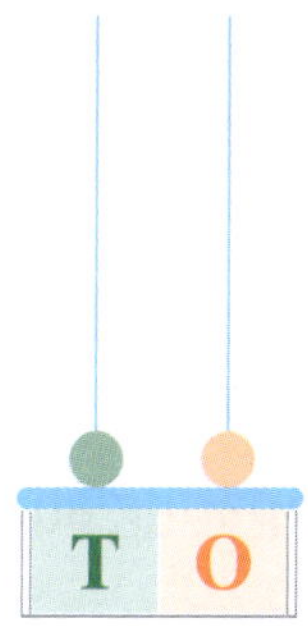

____

6. Write the following numbers in the increasing order.

a. 3, 9, 19, 6, 8 ____________________

b. 15, 13, 11, 18, 20 ____________________

7. Write the following numbers in the decreasing order.

a. 7, 2, 13, 5, 9 ____________________

b. 19, 14, 17, 11, 15 ____________________

8. Circle the greatest number and cross out the smallest number.

a. 9 11 13 18 14

b. 13 12 20 2 15

c. 19 17 4 20 11

d. 15 16 17 18 19

9. Write <, > or = sign in the given blanks.

a. 12 ______ 17 b. 13 ______ 13 c. 19 ______ 20 d. 15 ______ 11

10. The pear in which position is coloured?

2 Numbers up to 99

Prior Knowledge

- Numbers from 1 to 20 and their number names
- Concept of zero
- Numbers that come before, after and between
- Comparing and ordering numbers up to 20
- Ordinal numbers

Learning Objectives

- Read and write 2-digit numbers
- Counting in tens
- Counting forwards and backwards
- Place value, face value and expanded form of a number
- Comparing and ordering numbers
- Forming the greatest and smallest 2-digit numbers

Let's Get Started

Look at the aquarium.

Count and write how many of these are there in the picture.

GROUPING TENS

10 Ones

1 Ten

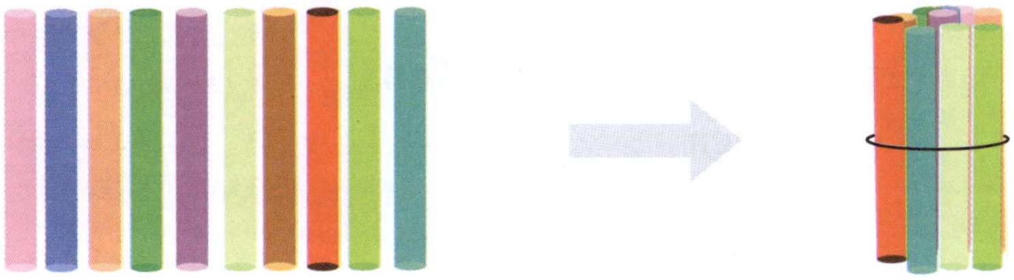

Ten ones when grouped together form one ten.

1 Ten is **10.**

10 is the smallest 2-digit number. To write 10, we need two places.

Tens	Ones
1	0

Counting in Tens

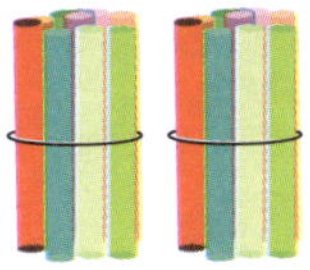

2 tens are twenty.

Tens	Ones
2	0

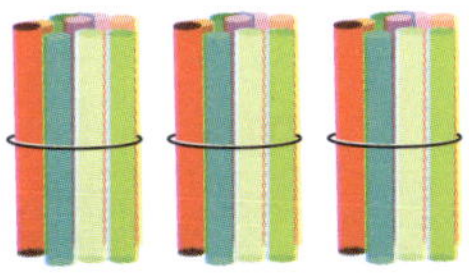

3 tens are thirty.

Tens	Ones
3	0

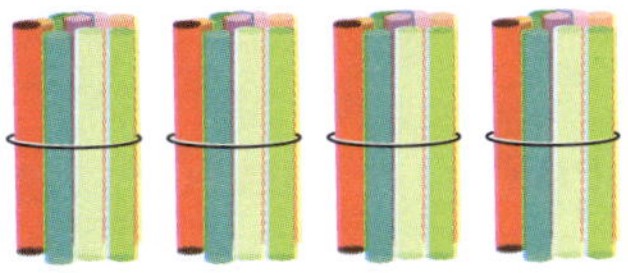

4 tens are forty.

Tens	Ones
4	0

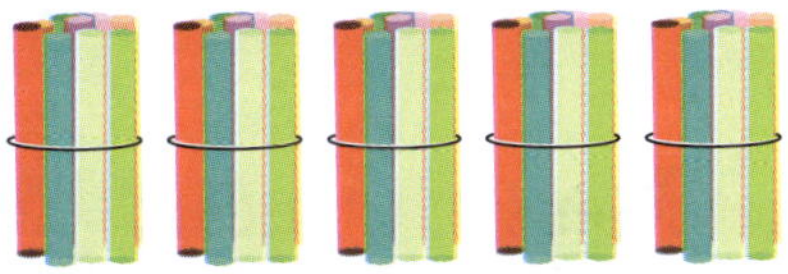

5 tens are fifty.

Tens	Ones
5	0

6 tens are sixty.

Tens	Ones
6	0

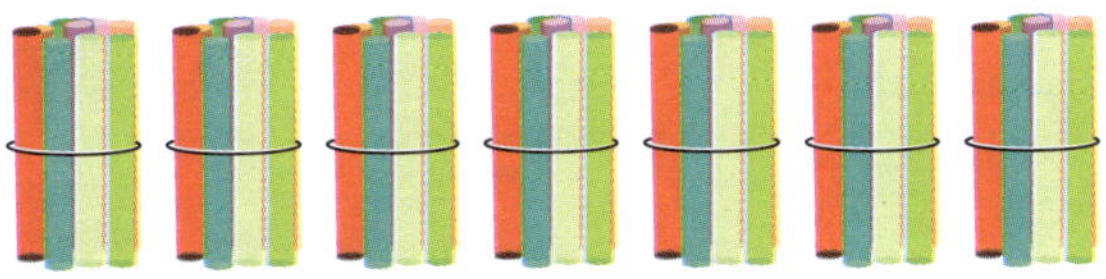

7 tens are seventy.

Tens	Ones
7	0

8 tens are eighty.

Tens	Ones
8	0

9 tens are ninety.

Tens	Ones
9	0

NUMBERS FROM 11 TO 20

Count and write the numbers and their names.

1 ten 1 one make 11 eleven

Tens	Ones
1	1

1 ten 2 ones make 12 twelve

Tens	Ones
1	2

1 ten 3 ones make ☐ ________

Tens	Ones

1 ten 4 ones make ☐ ________

Tens	Ones

1 ten 5 ones make ☐ ________

Tens	Ones

1 ten 6 ones make ☐ ________

Tens	Ones

1 ten 7 ones make ☐ ________

Tens	Ones

1 ten 8 ones make ☐ ________

Tens	Ones

1 ten 9 ones make ☐ ________

Tens	Ones

1 ten 10 ones make ☐ ________

Tens	Ones

NUMBERS FROM 21 TO 40

Count and write the numbers and their names.

2 tens 1 one make

Tens	Ones
2	1

twenty-one

2 tens 2 ones make

Tens	Ones
2	2

twenty-two

2 tens 3 ones make

Tens	Ones
2	3

twenty-three

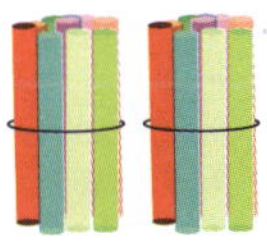 

2 tens 4 ones make

Tens	Ones

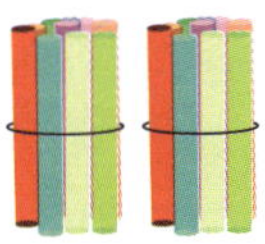 

2 tens 5 ones make

Tens	Ones

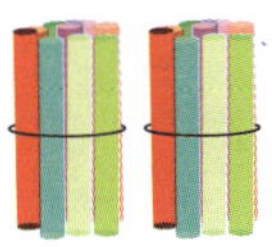 

2 tens 6 ones make

Tens	Ones

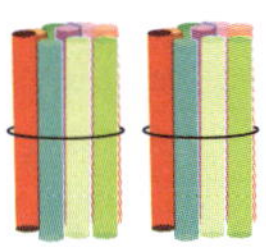 

2 tens 7 ones make

Tens	Ones

2 tens 8 ones make

Tens	Ones

2 tens 9 ones make

Tens	Ones

2 tens 10 ones make

Tens	Ones
3	0

thirty

3 tens

1 one make

Tens	Ones
3	1

thirty-one

3 tens

2 ones make

Tens	Ones
3	2

thirty-two

3 tens

3 ones make

Tens	Ones

3 tens

4 ones make

Tens	Ones

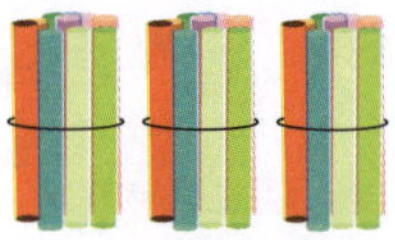

3 tens

5 ones make

Tens	Ones

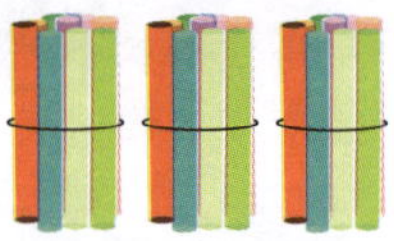

3 tens

6 ones make

Tens	Ones

3 tens

7 ones make

Tens	Ones

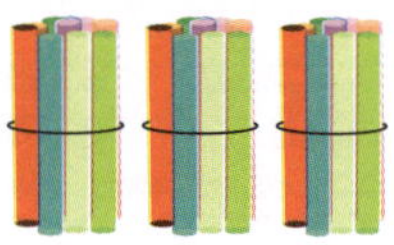

3 tens

8 ones make

Tens	Ones

3 tens

9 ones make

Tens	Ones

3 tens

10 ones make

Tens	Ones
4	0

forty

NUMBERS FROM 41 TO 60

Count and write the numbers and their names.

Tens	Ones
4	1

4 tens 1 one make forty-one

Tens	Ones

4 tens 2 ones make

Tens	Ones

4 tens 3 ones make

Tens	Ones

4 tens 4 ones make

Tens	Ones

4 tens 5 ones make

Tens	Ones

4 tens 6 ones make

Tens	Ones

4 tens 7 ones make

Tens	Ones

4 tens 8 ones make

Tens	Ones

4 tens 9 ones make

Tens	Ones

4 tens 10 ones make

5 tens 1 one make

Tens	Ones
5	1

fifty-one

5 tens 2 ones make

Tens	Ones

5 tens 3 ones make

Tens	Ones

5 tens 4 ones make

Tens	Ones

5 tens 5 ones make

Tens	Ones

5 tens 6 ones make

Tens	Ones

5 tens 7 ones make

Tens	Ones

5 tens 8 ones make

Tens	Ones

5 tens 9 ones make

Tens	Ones

5 tens 10 ones make

NUMBERS FROM 61 TO 80

Count and write the numbers and their names.

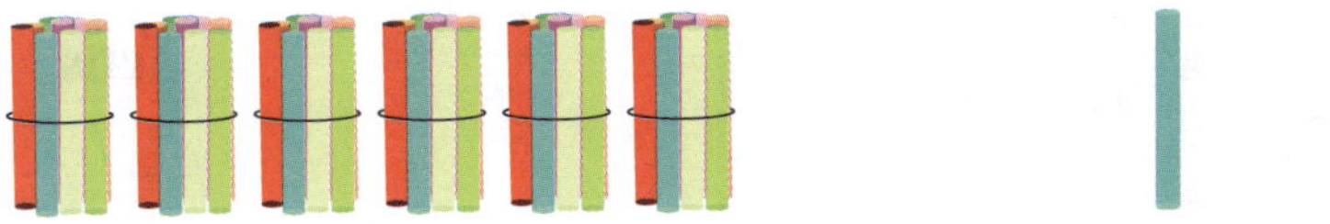

6 tens 1 one make

Tens	Ones
6	1

sixty-one

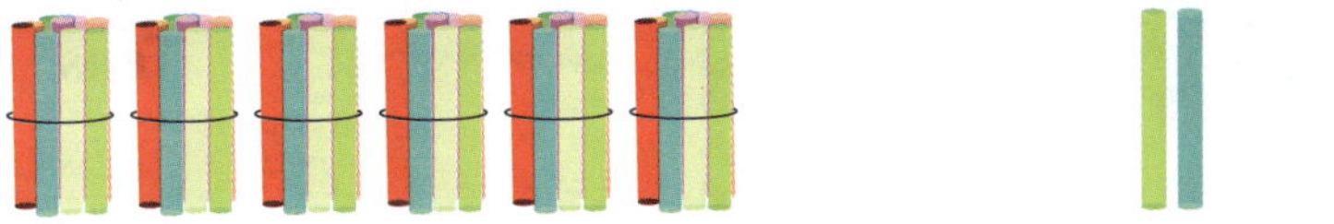

6 tens 2 ones make

Tens	Ones

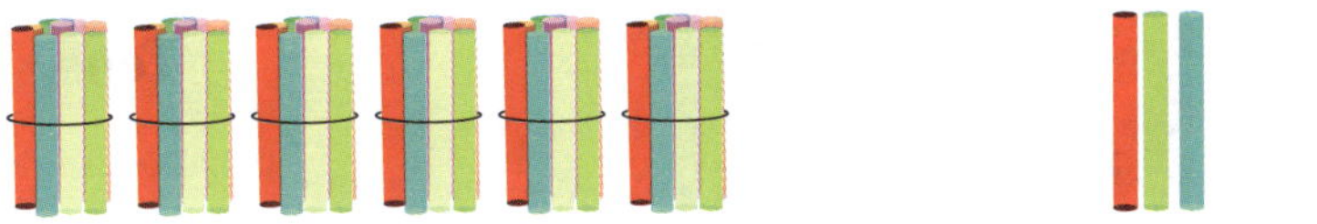

6 tens 3 ones make

Tens	Ones

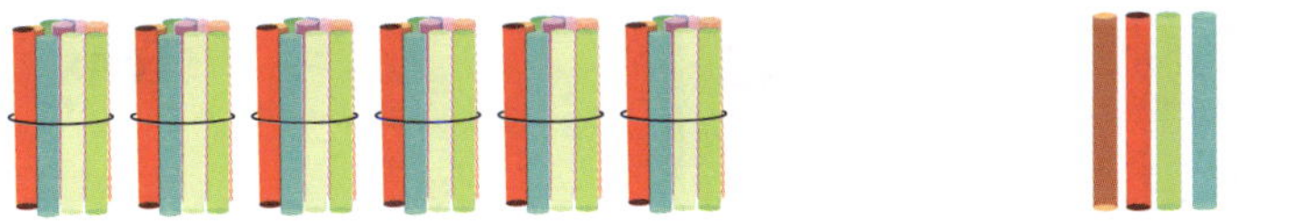

6 tens 4 ones make

Tens	Ones

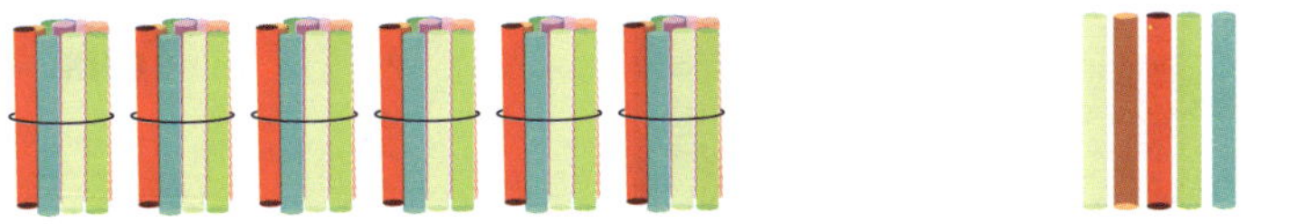

6 tens 5 ones make

Tens	Ones

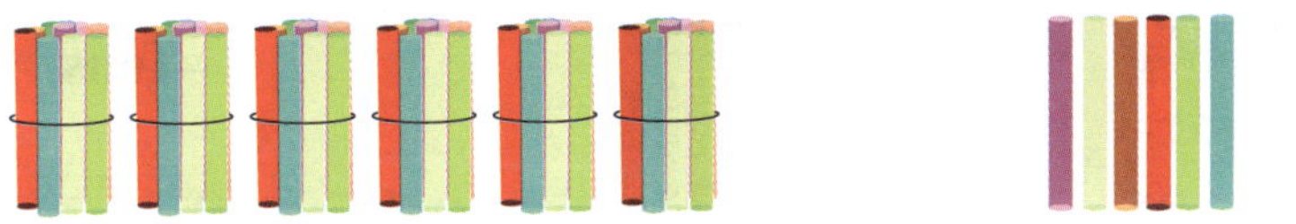

6 tens 6 ones make

Tens	Ones

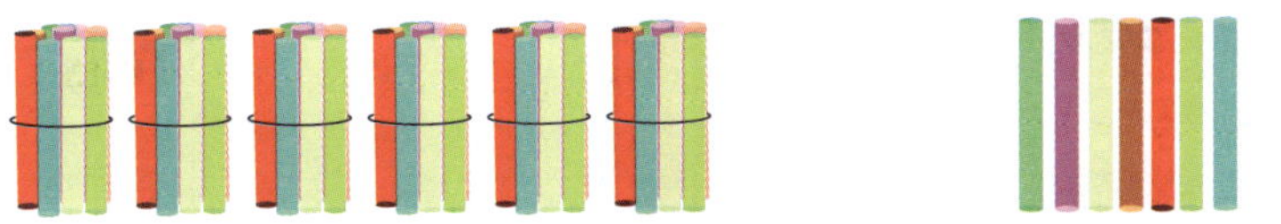

6 tens 7 ones make

Tens	Ones

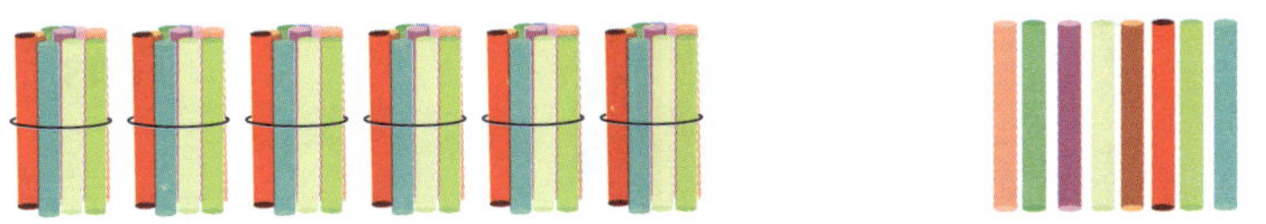

6 tens 8 ones make

Tens	Ones

6 tens 9 ones make

Tens	Ones

6 tens 10 ones make

Tens	Ones

7 tens 1 one make

Tens	Ones
7	1

seventy-one

7 tens 2 ones make

Tens	Ones

7 tens 3 ones make

Tens	Ones

7 tens 4 ones make

Tens	Ones

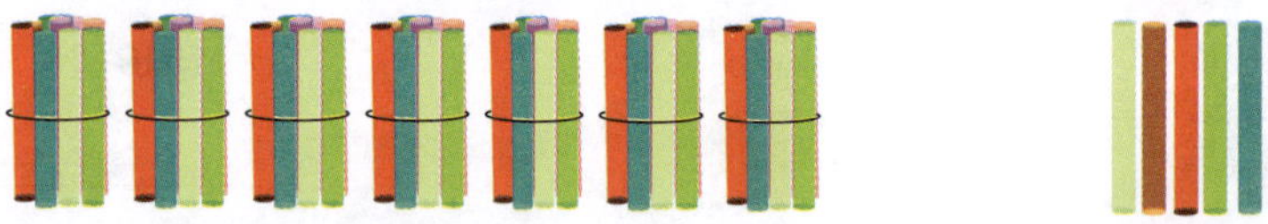

7 tens 5 ones make

Tens	Ones

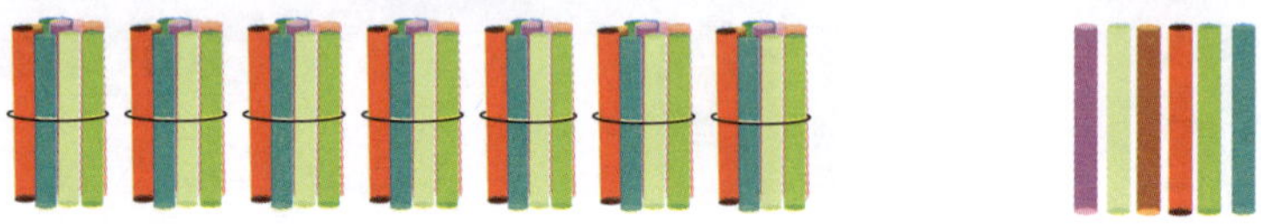

7 tens 6 ones make

Tens	Ones

7 tens 7 ones make

Tens	Ones

7 tens 8 ones make

Tens	Ones

7 tens 9 ones make

Tens	Ones

7 tens 10 ones make

Tens	Ones

NUMBERS FROM 81 TO 99

Count and write the numbers and their names.

8 tens 1 one make

Tens	Ones
8	1

eighty-one

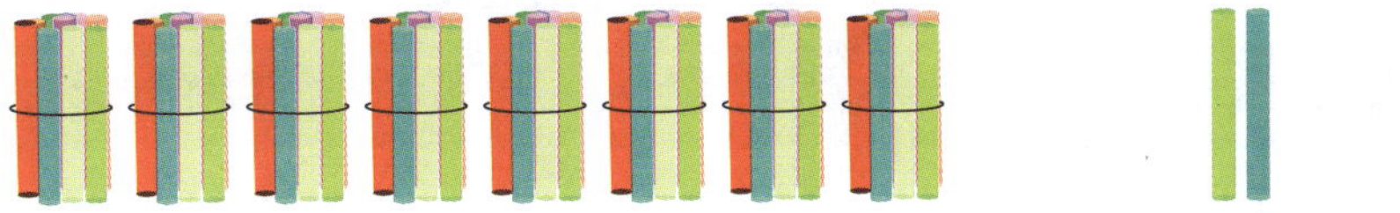

8 tens 2 ones make

Tens	Ones

8 tens 3 ones make

Tens	Ones

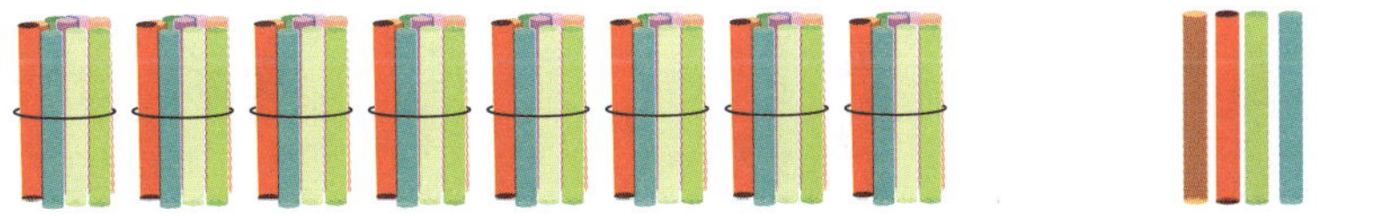

8 tens 4 ones make

Tens	Ones

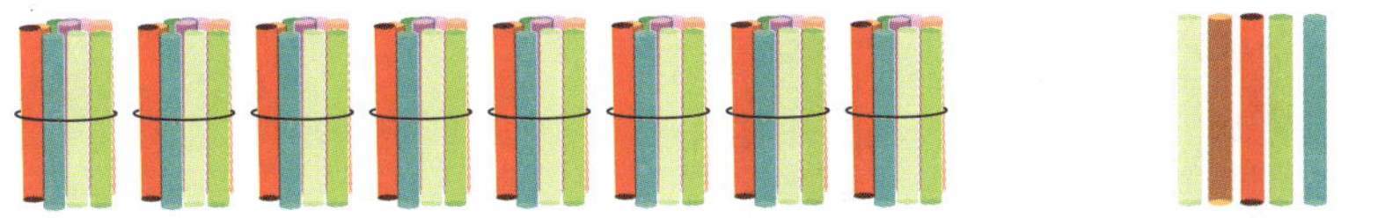

8 tens 5 ones make

Tens	Ones

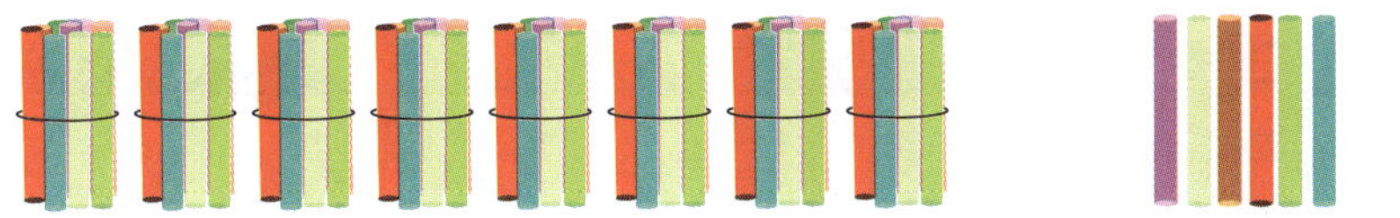

8 tens 6 ones make

Tens	Ones

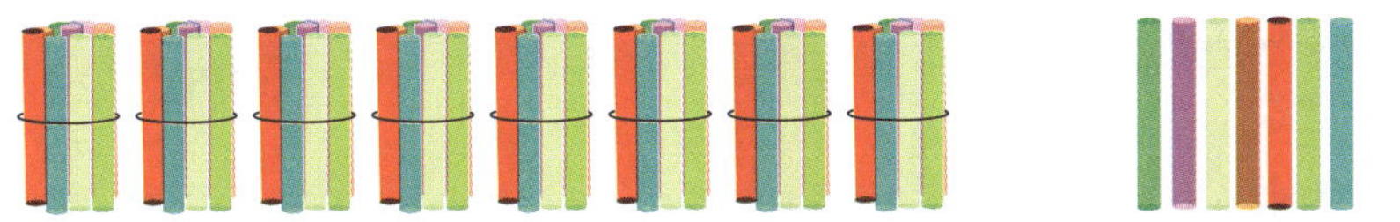

8 tens 7 ones make

Tens	Ones

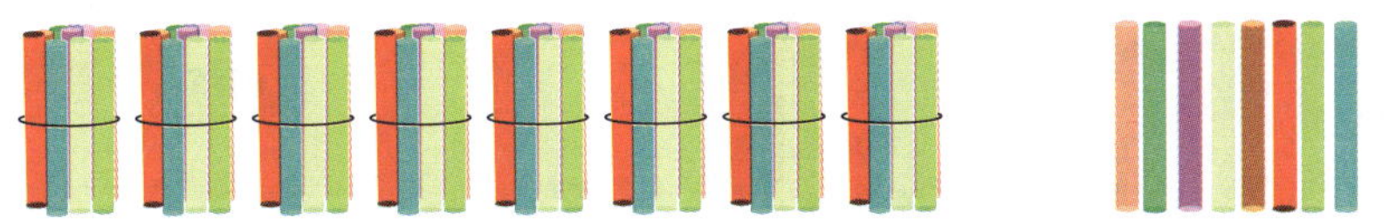

8 tens 8 ones make

Tens	Ones

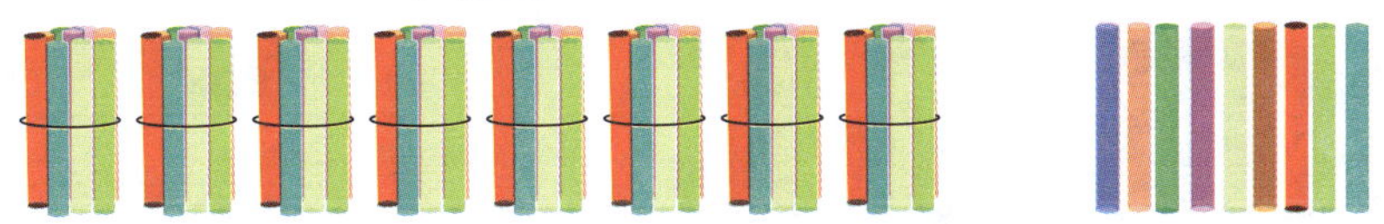

8 tens 9 ones make

Tens	Ones

8 tens 10 ones make

Tens	Ones

9 tens 1 one make

Tens	Ones
9	1

ninety-one

9 tens 2 ones make

Tens	Ones

9 tens 3 ones make

Tens	Ones

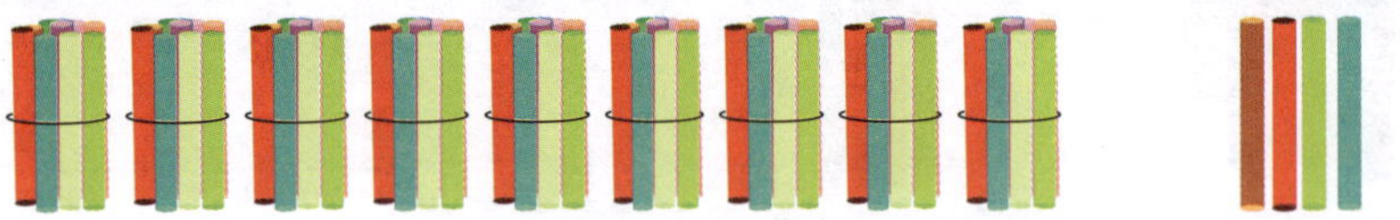

9 tens 4 ones make

Tens	Ones

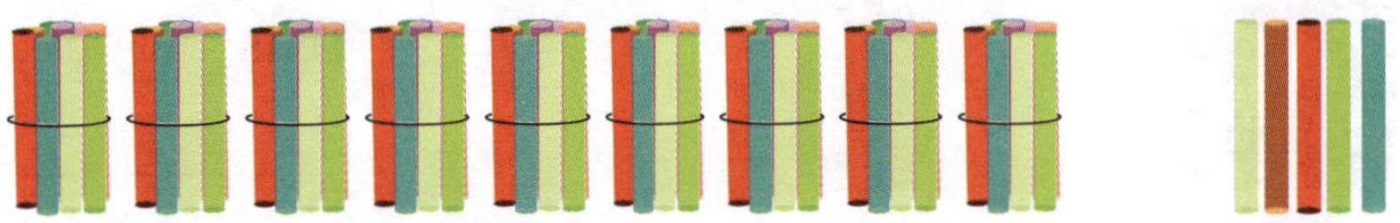

9 tens 5 ones make

Tens	Ones

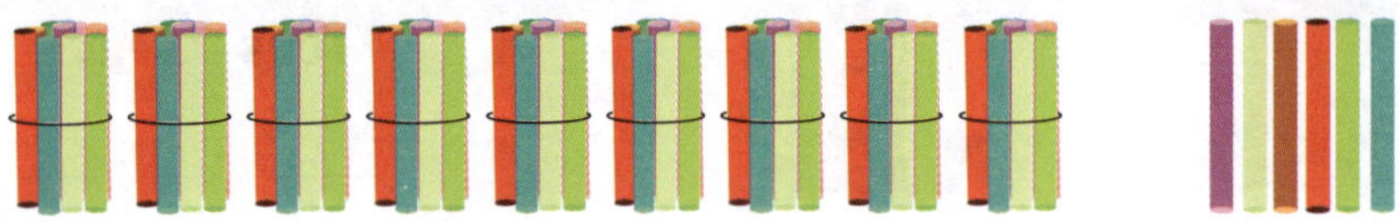

9 tens 6 ones make

Tens	Ones

9 tens 7 ones make

Tens	Ones

9 tens 8 ones make

Tens	Ones

9 tens 9 ones make

Tens	Ones

9 tens 10 ones make

100

hundred

REPRESENTING NUMBERS ON THE ABACUS

Example 1: Represent the number 45 on abacus.

Solution: 45 is equal to 4 tens 5 ones.

Example 2: Represent the number 134 on abacus.

Solution: 134 is equal to 1 hundred 3 tens 4 ones.

EXERCISE 2.1

Fill in the blanks. Also, draw the beads on the abacus.

1.

T	O
2	3

= _____ tens _____ ones

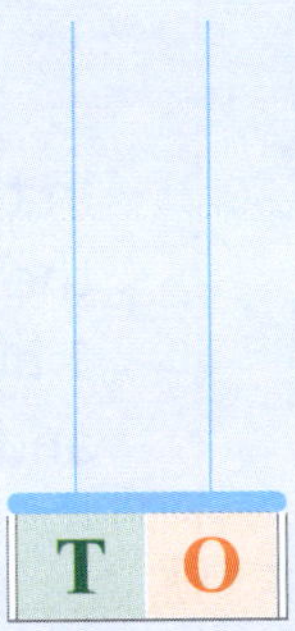

2.

T	O
3	7

= _____ tens _____ ones

3.

T	O
4	3

= _____ tens _____ ones

4.

T	O
5	6

= _____ tens _____ ones

5.

H	T	O
1	6	5

= ___ hundred ___ tens ___ ones

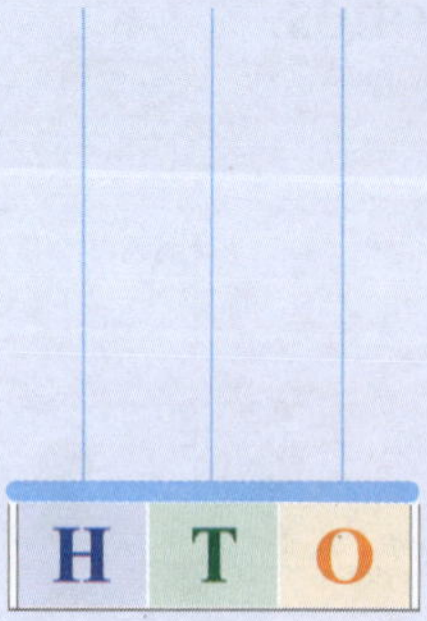

6.

H	T	O
2	3	8

= ___ hundreds ___ tens ___ ones

PLACE VALUE AND FACE VALUE

Place Value

The place value is the position or place of a digit in a number. The place value of a digit is the digit followed by the number of zeros in the value of that place.

T	O
5	4

In this, the place value of 5 is 50 or 5 tens.
The place value of 4 is 4 or 4 ones.

So, 54 = 50 + 4

T	O
8	0

In this, the place value of 8 is 80 or 8 tens.
The place value of 0 is 0 or 0 ones.

So, 80 = 80 + 0

H	T	O
1	6	7

In the number 167, the place value of 1 is 1 hundred, 6 is 6 tens and 7 is 7 ones.

So, 100 + 60 + 7 = 167.

Face Value

In any given number, the face value of a digit is the digit itself.

T	O
5	4

In this, the face value of 5 is 5.
The face value of 4 is 4.

T	O
8	0

In this, the face value of 8 is 8.
The face value of 0 is 0.

REMEMBER

- The place value and the face value of zero are always zero.
- For a digit in ones place, the place value is same as the face value.
- **Expanded form** is the standard form of the numbers. For example, 67 = 60 + 7

Exercise 2.2

1. Write the place values of each digit. Also write their names.

a. 23

b. 40

c. 69

d. 87

e. 37

f. 53

g. 72

h. 99

2. Write the face values of each digit.

a. 48

b. 79

c. 51

d. 90

e. 28

f. 65

g. 83

h. 92

3. Fill in the blanks.

a. 8 tens and 2 ones make ____.

b. 7 tens and 9 ones make ____.

c. 5 tens and 3 ones make ____.

d. 4 tens and 1 one make ____.

e. 6 tens and 7 ones make ____.

f. 3 tens and 9 ones make ____.

4. **Write the following numbers as tens and ones.**

a. 23 = ___ tens and ___ ones b. 50 = ____ tens and ____ones

c. 30 = ___ tens and ___ ones d. 45 = ____ tens and ____ ones

e. 71 = ___ tens and ___ one f. 88 = _____ tens and ____ ones

FORWARD AND BACKWARD COUNTING

When counting forwards, each number is one more than the previous number.

Example 3: Count forward from 32.

32, _____, _____, _____, _____, _____

Solution: 32, 33, 34, 35, 36, 37

When counting backwards, each number is one less than the previous number.

Example 4: Count backward from 75.

75, _____, _____, _____, _____, _____

Solution: 75, 74, 73, 72, 71, 70

Exercise 2.3

1. **Write the next four numbers.**

a. Starting from 5

____, ____, ____, ____, ____

b. Starting from 27

____, ____, ____, ____, ____

c. Starting from 39

____, ____, ____, ____, ____

d. Starting from 52

____, ____, ____, ____, ____

e. Starting from 75

____, ____, ____, ____, ____

f. Starting from 82

____, ____, ____, ____, ____

2. **Fill in the missing numbers by counting forward or backward.**

a. 25, ____, ____, 28, ____, ____ b. 36, ____, ____, ____, 32, ____

c. 48, ____, ____, 51, ____, ____ d. 58, ____, 56, ____, ____, ____

e. 63, ____, ____, ____, 67, ____ f. 74, ____, ____, ____, 70, ____

g. 80, ____, ____, ____, ____, 85 h. 92, ____, ____, ____, ____, 87

BEFORE, AFTER AND IN BETWEEN

Consider the three numbers, 55, 56 and 57.

55	56	57

55 comes just before 56.   57 comes just after 56.   56 is in between 55 and 57.

EXERCISE 2.4

1. **Write the number that comes just before.**

   a. ☐ 19   b. ☐ 28   c. ☐ 37   d. ☐ 45

   e. ☐ 58   f. ☐ 63   g. ☐ 79   h. ☐ 82

   i. ☐ 99   j. ☐ 91

2. **Write the number that comes just after.**

   a. 30 ☐   b. 17 ☐   c. 24 ☐   d. 32 ☐

   e. 49 ☐   f. 55 ☐   g. 61 ☐   h. 78 ☐

   i. 82 ☐   j. 98 ☐

3. **Write the numbers that come in between.**

   a. 23, ☐, 25   b. 36, ☐, ☐, 39

   c. 47, ☐, ☐, ☐, 51   d. 62, ☐, ☐, ☐, ☐, 67

   e. 73, ☐, ☐, 76   f. 90, ☐, ☐, ☐, ☐, 95

COMPARING AND ORDERING NUMBERS

Example 5: Which is greater: 34 or 21?

Solution: Compare the tens.

3 tens is more than 2 tens.

So, 34 is greater than 21.

34 > 21

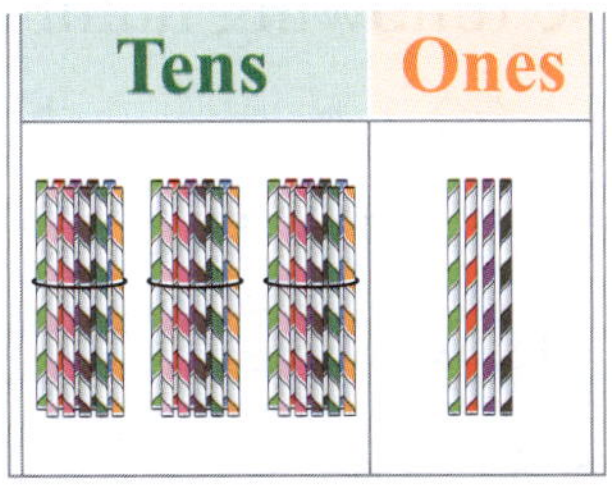

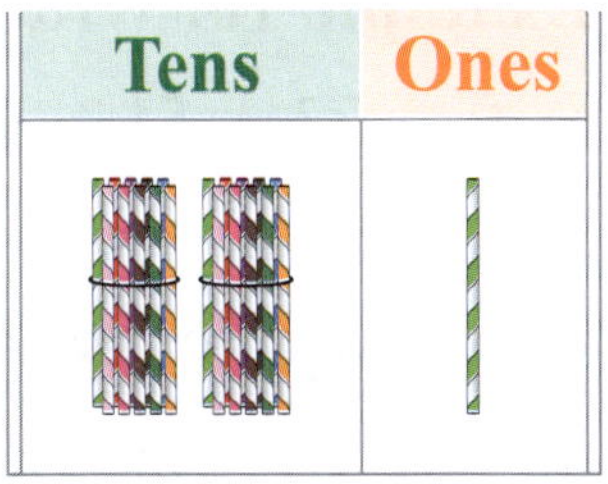

Example 6: Which is smaller: 53 or 59?

Solution: Here, the tens are the same.

So, compare the ones.

3 ones is less than 9 ones.

So, 53 is smaller than 59.

53 < 59

Example 7: Circle the greatest number out of the following.

32, 9, 65, 15, 71

Solution: As 71 > 65 > 32 > 15 > 9.

So, 71 is the greatest number.

Therefore, 32, 9, 65, 15, (71)

Example 8: Circle the smallest number out of the following.

18, 93, 29, 47, 54

Solution: As 18 < 29 < 47 < 54 < 93.

So, 18 is the smallest number.

Therefore, (18), 93, 29, 47, 54

Increasing Order and Decreasing Order

In increasing order, we write numbers from the smallest to the greatest.
In decreasing order, we write numbers from the greatest to the smallest.

Example 9: Write the following numbers in the increasing order.

a. 72, 61, 15, 84, 40 b. 46, 5, 79, 18, 33

Solution: a. As 15 < 40 < 61 < 72 < 84.

Therefore, 15, 40, 61, 72, 84

b. As 5 < 18 < 33 < 46 < 79.

Therefore, 5, 18, 33, 46, 79

Example 10: Write the following numbers in the decreasing order.

a. 9, 73, 51, 18, 79 b. 4, 69, 72, 51, 80

Solution: a. As 79 > 73 > 51 > 18 > 9

Therefore, 79, 73, 51, 18, 9

b. As 80 > 72 > 69 > 51 > 4.

Therefore, 80, 72, 69, 51, 4

FORMING NUMBERS USING THE GIVEN DIGITS

Number cards from 0 to 9 are given below.

0	1	2	3	4	5	6	7	8	9

We can use any two digits to form 2-digit numbers. The two digits could be different or the same.

Without Repetition

Let us take two digits, 2 and 5.
We can form two different numbers depending on the order we place these digits.

52	25

With Repetition

Let us take two digits, 7 and 9.
We can form the following numbers by repeating the same digit.

99	77

REMEMBER

- To form the greatest 2-digit number without repetition, we write the greatest digit first and then the smallest digit.
- To form the smallest 2-digit number without repetition, we write the smallest digit first followed by the greatest digit.
- If 0 comes in the tens place, then it will be a 1-digit number.

EXERCISE 2.5

1. Fill in the boxes with >, < or =.

a. 49 ☐ 11 b. 86 ☐ 87 c. 35 ☐ 35

d. 59 ☐ 61 e. 40 ☐ 40 f. 61 ☐ 23

g. 82 ☐ 82 h. 88 ☐ 91 i. 80 ☐ 60

2. Circle ◯ the greatest number. Tick (✓) the smallest number.

a.

39	18	96	8	52

b.

5	76	13	81	23

c.

62	9	47	21	30

d.

8	98	21	18	99

e.

35	19	83	2	99

f.

72	43	29	85	60

3. **Write the following numbers in the increasing order.**

a. 92, 45, 38, 16, 70

____, ____, ____, ____, ____

b. 79, 15, 58, 41, 90

____, ____, ____, ____, ____

c. 30, 61, 28, 47, 99

____, ____, ____, ____, ____

4. **Write the following numbers in the decreasing order.**

a. 73, 48, 25, 12, 60

____, ____, ____, ____, ____

b. 80, 19, 35, 62, 41

____, ____, ____, ____, ____

c. 12, 90, 53, 64, 27

____, ____, ____, ____, ____

5. **Colour the numbers as instructed.**

a. Numbers greater than 74

70	71	72	73	74	75	76	77	78

b. Numbers smaller than 49

43	44	45	46	47	48	49	50	51	52

6. **Form the greatest and the smallest 2-digit numbers from the given digits.**

a. without repetition

i. 5 and 9

Greatest	Smallest

ii. 3 and 7

Greatest	Smallest

b. with repetition

i. 6 and 1

Greatest	Smallest

ii. 4 and 8

Greatest	Smallest

Key Concepts

Numbers up to 99

Count, read and write

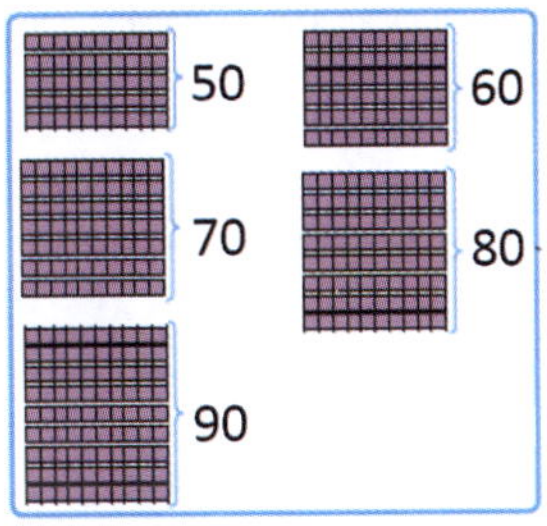

50 Fifty 60 Sixty
70 Seventy 80 Eight
90 Ninety

Place value, face value and expanded form

26 = 2 tens 6 ones
20 + 6 = 26

Forward and backward counting

Forward counting
3, 4, 5, 6, 7, 8

Backward counting
7, 6, 5, 4, 3, 2

Compare and order numbers

48 56 59

Number with bigger digit in tens is bigger.

Therefore, 48 < 56 and 48 < 59

Number with bigger digit in the ones place is bigger when the digits in tens are the same.

56 < 59

Therefore, 48 < 56 < 59

Forming numbers

Smallest and greatest numbers formed using the digits;

3 and 5

i. without repetition: 35 and 53
ii. with repetition: 33 and 55

Revision Exercise

1. Choose the correct option.

a. The name of the number 86 is

i. twenty-eight ii. sixty-eight iii. eighty-six iv. sixteen

b. Which number is greater than 47?

i. 42 ii. 49 iii. 45 iv. 40

c. Which number is smaller than 65?

i. 64 ii. 66 iii. 68 iv. 69

d. Which number lies between 34 and 42?

i. 50 ii. 40 iii. 30 iv. 20

2. Write the number names of each of the following numbers.

a. 21 ____________ b. 39 ____________

c. 63 ____________ d. 92 ____________

3. Count the following and write the answers.

a.

____ tens and ____ ones make ____

b.

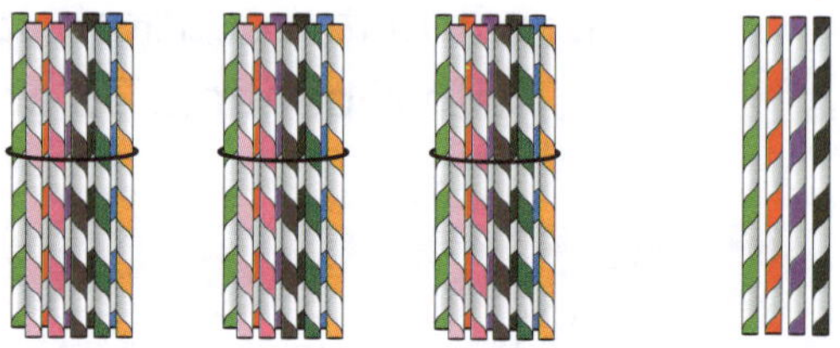

____ tens and ____ ones make ____

4. Fill in the blanks.

a. 56 = ____ tens and ____ ones

b. 72 = ____ tens and ____ ones

c. 49 = ____ tens and ____ ones

d. 23 = ____ tens and ____ ones

5. **Fill in the numbers that come between the given numbers.**

a. 42, ______, 44 b. 55, ______, ______, 58

c. 86, ______, ______, 89 d. 67, ______, ______, ______, 71

6. **Fill in the blanks with >, < or =.**

a. 92 ____ 86 b. 23 ____ 49 c. 29 ____ 52

d. 81 ____ 94 e. 63 ____ 63 f. 53 ____ 95

7. **Fill in the blanks.**

a. 5 tens and 1 one make ______

b. 4 tens and 6 ones make ______

c. 2 tens and 4 ones make ______

d. 1 ten and 8 ones make ______

8. **Draw the beads on the abacus for 64. Also, for 64, write the place value and face value of 6 in the given space.**

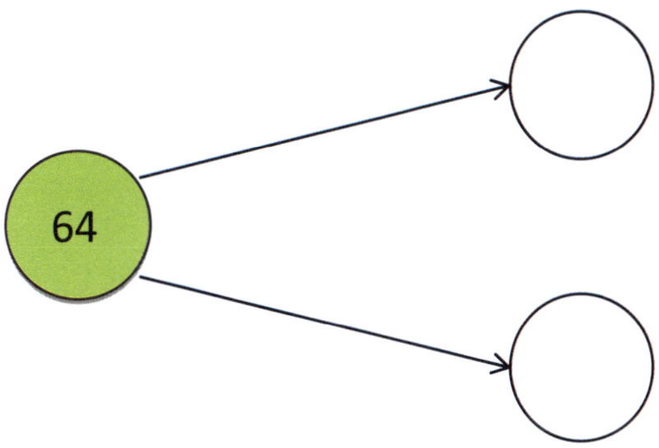

Place value

Face value

9. **Circle all the numbers smaller than 65.**

74		39
	91	
23		47

10. **Write the 2-digit numbers formed by the following numbers, with or without repetition.**

a. 8 and 9 b. 4 and 2 c. 7 and 9 d. 5 and 6

3 Addition up to 20

Prior Knowledge

- Counting from 1 to 20
- Forward and backward counting

Learning Objectives

- Addition till 20
- Number combinations
- Applying addition facts
- Addition on a number line
- Vertical addition
- Addition of three numbers
- Addition of 2-digit numbers with 1-digit number
- Solving word problems on addition

Let's Get Started

Circle the correct number of objects.

4 8 9

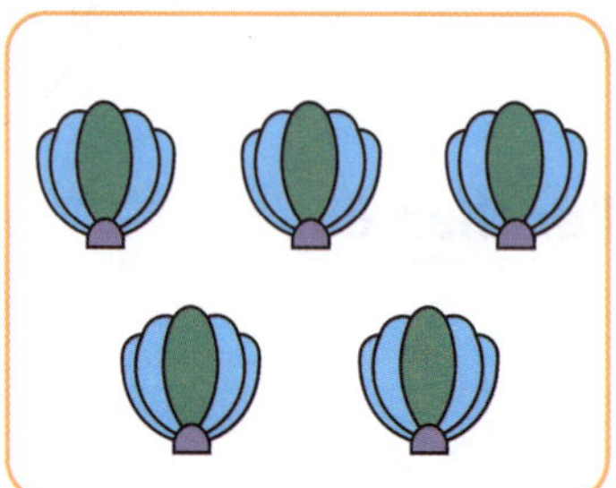

6 7 5

2 3 4

1 3 5

10 12 8

9 11 7

INTRODUCTION TO ADDITION

Riya has 4 blue balls and 2 green balls. Let us find the total number of balls.

4 balls and 2 balls make 6 balls

There are 6 balls in total.

Putting things together is called **addition**.

We use the sign '+' to show addition. This symbol is read as **plus**.

So, 4 balls + 2 balls = 6 balls

It is read as 4 plus 2 is equal to 6.

EXERCISE 3.1

Count the objects and find the sums.

1. 

   ______ + ______ = ______

2. 

   ______ + ______ = ______

3. 

   ______ + ______ = ______

4. 

   ______ + ______ = ______

5. 

   ______ + ______ = ______

NUMBER COMBINATIONS

Any number can be represented as a combination of numbers. These are called **number combinations**. Let us have a look at the number combinations of the following numbers.

Combinations of 1

1 + 0 = 1

0 + 1 = 1

Combinations of 2

2 + 0 = 2

1 + 1 = 2

0 + 2 = 2

Combinations of 3

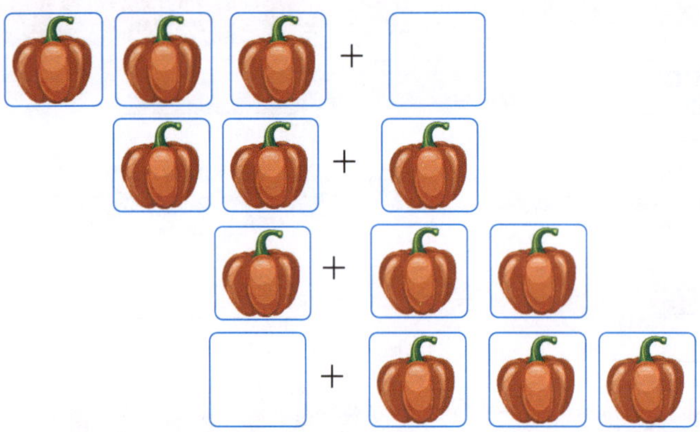

3 + 0 = 3

2 + 1 = 3

1 + 2 = 3

0 + 3 = 3

Combinations of 4

4 + 0 = 4

3 + 1 = 4

2 + 2 = 4

1 + 3 = 4

0 + 4 = 4

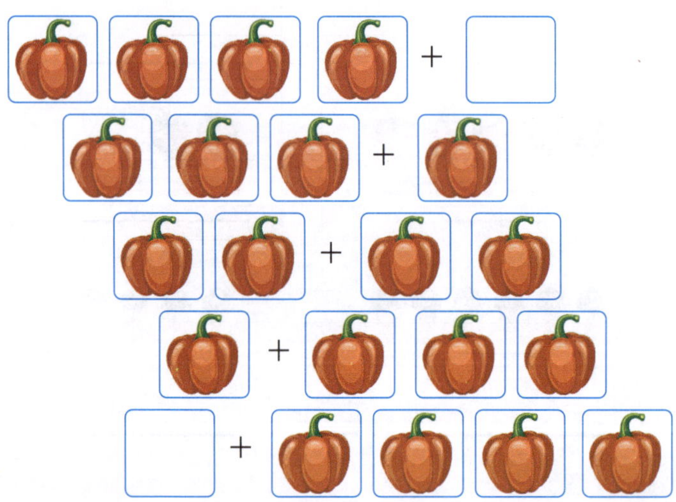

Combinations of 5

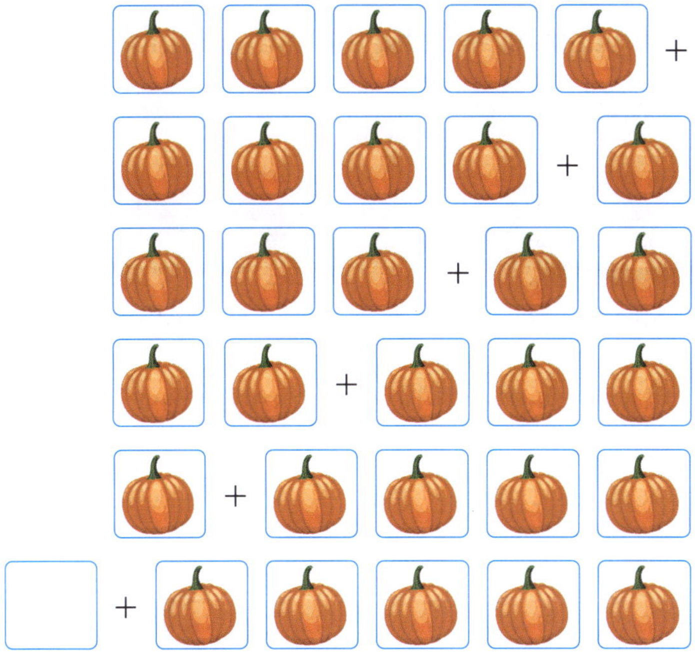

5 + 0 = 5

4 + 1 = 5

3 + 2 = 5

2 + 3 = 5

1 + 4 = 5

0 + 5 = 5

EXERCISE 3.2

Write the number combinations of 7. One has been done for you.

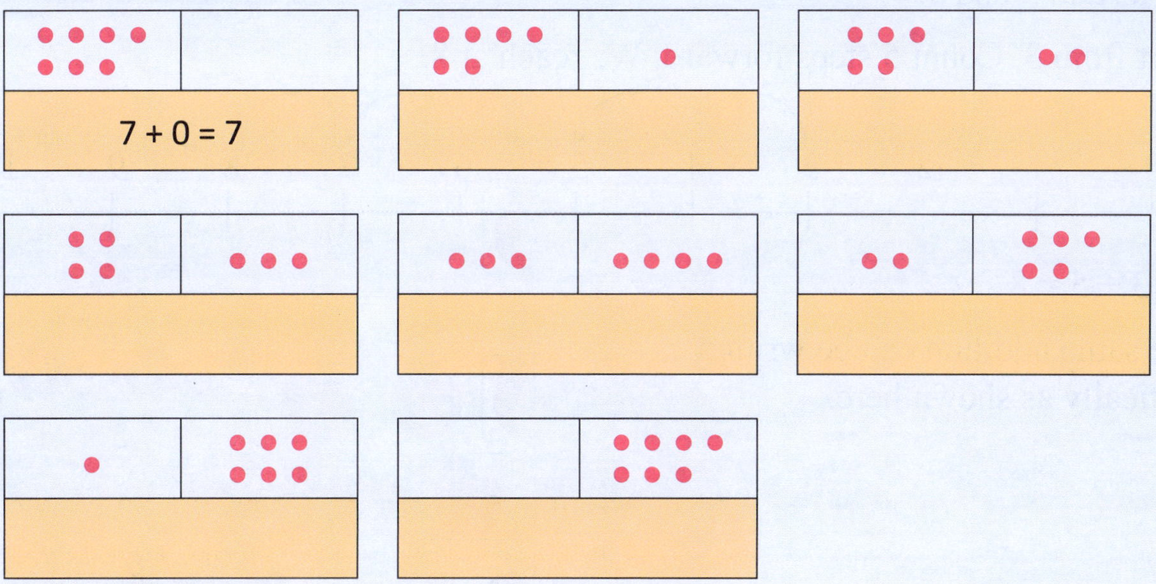

ADDITION FACTS

Fact 1: If we add 0 (zero) to a number, the answer will be the same number. Its value does not change.

5 apples + 0 apple = 5 apples

Fact 2: If we add 1 (one) to a number, the answer will be the number just after the given number. Its value increases by 1.

6 candles + 1 candle = 7 candles

ADDITION BY FORWARD COUNTING

Let us add 3 and 5.

Start from 3. Count 5 steps forward. We reach at 8.

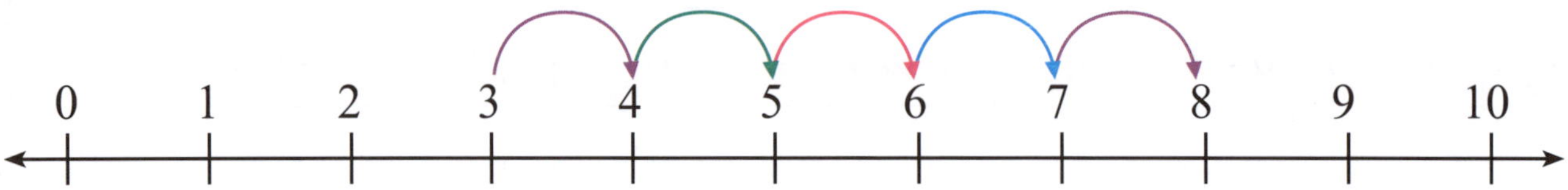

So, $3 + 5 = 8$

The same addition can be written vertically as shown here.

	O
	3
+	5
	8

We can count on our fingers too.

Count 3 on your little finger and then count 5 on your index and middle fingers.

The total dots give the sum of the numbers, that is, $3 + 5 = 8$.

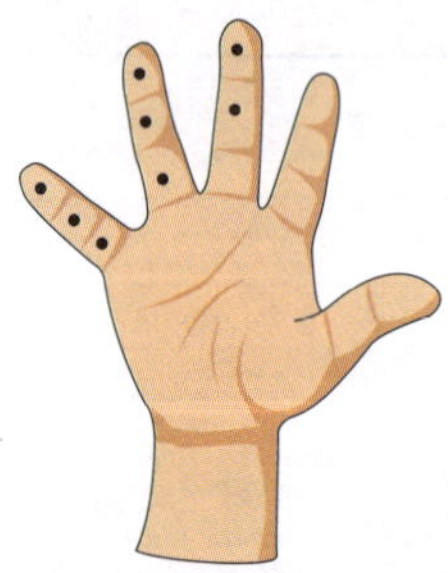

ADDITION OF THREE NUMBERS

Let us learn to add three numbers.

Horizontal Addition

5 + 2 + 1

= 7 + 1

= 8

> Begin by adding the first two numbers. Then add the third number to the answer of the first addition.

Vertical Addition

5	
2	→ 7
+ 1	→ 8
8	

So, $5 + 2 + 1 = 8$

REMEMBER

We can add numbers in any order and still get the same answer. For example, $6 + 3 = 3 + 6 = 9$

EXERCISE 3.3

1. Add the following numbers.

a. 1 + 1 = ☐ b. 2 + 0 = ☐ c. 4 + 1 = ☐

d. 3 + 1 = ☐ e. 0 + 4 = ☐ f. 10 + 0 = ☐

2. Fill in the blanks.

a. 3 + 5 = 5 + ☐ b. 4 + 6 = ☐ + 4

c. 9 + 0 = 0 + ☐ d. 1 + 2 = ☐ + 1

3. Add the following on the given number lines.

a. 3 + 1 = ☐

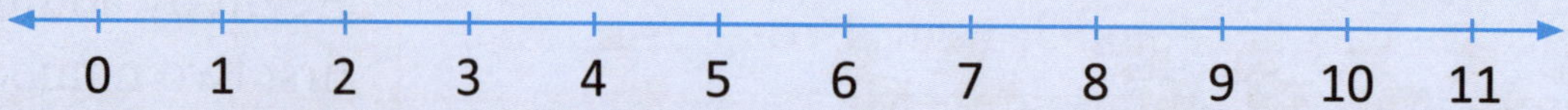

b. 6 + 2 = ☐

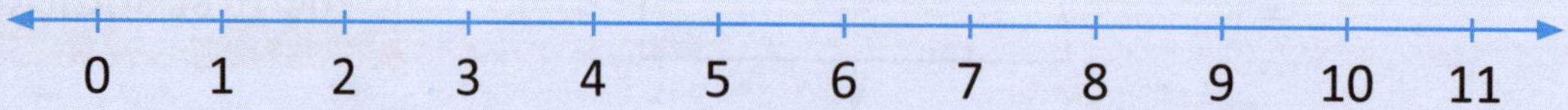

c. 16 + 1 = ☐

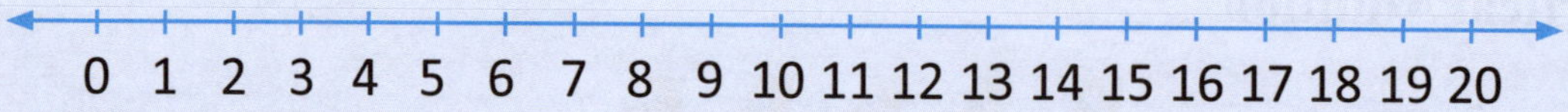

d. 5 + 4 + 2 = ☐

4. Add the following numbers.

a.
```
  2
  3
+ 1
---
```
2 + 3 + 1 = ____

b.
```
  4
  2
+ 3
---
```
4 + 2 + 3 = ____

c.
```
  6
  2
+ 2
---
```
6 + 2 + 2 = ____

d.
```
  5
  3
+ 4
---
```
5 + 3 + 4 = ____

e.
```
  1
  9
+ 3
---
```
1 + 9 + 3 = ____

f.
```
  8
  2
+ 7
---
```
8 + 2 + 7 = ____

g.
```
  5
  3
+ 7
---
```
5 + 3 + 7 = ____

h.
```
  9
  3
+ 1
---
```
9 + 3 + 1 = ____

i.
```
  6
  4
+ 5
---
```
6 + 4 + 5 = ____

j.
```
  8
  8
+ 2
---
```
8 + 8 + 2 = ____

k.
```
  7
  5
+ 1
---
```
7 + 5 + 1 = ____

l.
```
  4
  6
+ 3
---
```
4 + 6 + 3 = ____

ADDITION OF 2-DIGIT NUMBERS WITH 1-DIGIT NUMBERS

Example 1: Solve 14 + 3.

Solution: To add 14 and 3, write 14 as a 2-digit number. Write 3 as a single-digit number in the ones place. Now add the two numbers as shown alongside.

Thus, 14 + 3 = 17.

	T	O
	1	4
+		3
	1	7

EXERCISE 3.4

Add the following numbers.

1.

	T	O
	1	3
+		2

2.

	T	O
	1	5
+		4

3.

	T	O
	1	1
+		7

4.

	T	O
	1	4
+		1

5.

	T	O
	1	6
+		3

6.

	T	O
	1	3
+		5

7.

	T	O
	1	7
+		2

8.

	T	O
	1	8
+		0

9.

	T	O
	1	1
+		2

10.

	T	O
	1	2
+		7

WORD PROBLEMS

Example 2: I have 3 red marbles and 2 blue marbles. How many marbles do I have in total?

Solution:

red marbles

blue marbles

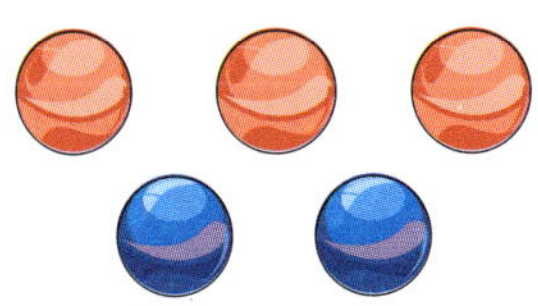

3 + 2 = 5

Thus, I have 5 marbles in total.

Example 3: Seema read 6 pages of a story book on Monday, 2 pages on Tuesday and 7 pages on Wednesday. How many pages did Seema read in all?

Solution:

Number of pages Seema read on Monday = 6

Number of pages Seema read on Tuesday = 2

Number of pages Seema read on Wednesday = 7

Total number of pages Seema read = 6 + 2 + 7 = 15

Thus, Seema read 15 pages in all.

	T	O
		6
		2
+		7
	1	5

Exercise 3.5

Solve the following word problems.

1. Zahir bought 4 mugs yesterday and 3 mugs today. How many mugs did Zahir buy in two days?

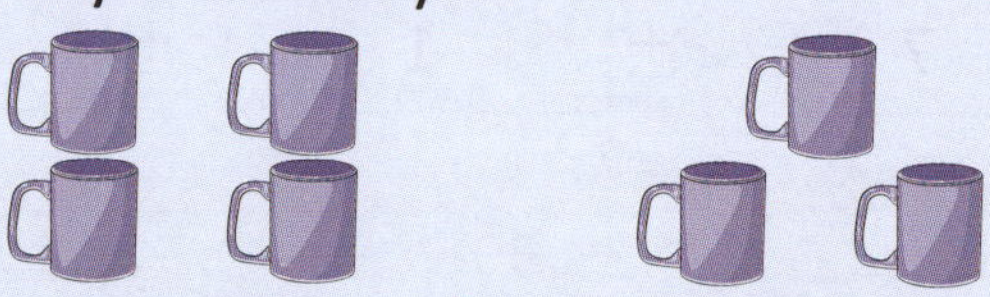

____ + ____ = ____

Thus, Zahir bought ____ mugs in two days.

2. Kia drank 4 glasses of water before lunch. She drank 4 glasses of water after lunch. How many glasses of water did she drink in total?

____ + ____ = ____

Thus, Kia drank ____ glasses of water.

3. Three children are playing. Two more children join them. How many children are playing in all?

____ + ____ = ____

Thus, there are ____ children playing in all.

4. Sunil has 7 hats, 6 balls and 3 balloons. How many objects does Sunil have in all?

	T	O
+		

Thus, Sunil has ☐ objects in all.

Key Concepts

Addition up to 20

Addition facts

- When we add zero to a number, we get the number itself.
  12 + 0 = 12
- When we add 1 to a number, we get the next number.
  12 + 1 = 13

Adding two 1-digit numbers

Add 5 + 3.
Count forward from 5.
5, 6, 7, 8
5 + 3 = 8
also, 3 + 5 = 8

Adding 2-digit number and 1-digit number

Add 11 + 4.

$$\begin{array}{r} 11 \\ +\ \ 4 \\ \hline 15 \\ \hline \end{array}$$

Adding three 1-digit numbers

Add 6 + 4 + 7.
First add, 6 and 4.
6 + 4 = 10
Now, add 7 to it.
10 + 7 = 17
So, 6 + 4 + 7 = 17
Also, 4 + 6 + 7 = 17,
7 + 4 + 6 = 17

Revision Exercise

1. Circle the correct answer in each of the following.

a.

	T	O
	1	3
+		5

20
18
15

b.

	T	O
	1	7
+		0

10
13
17

c.

	O
	7
	1
+	0

10
8
19

d.

	T	O
		3
		4
+		3

10
12
18

2. Add the following numbers on the number line.

a. 7 + 8

0 1 2 3 4 5 6 7 8 9 10 11 12 13 14 15 16 17 18 19 20

b. 2 + 6 + 3

0 1 2 3 4 5 6 7 8 9 10 11 12 13 14 15 16 17 18 19 20

3. There are 8 students in a dance academy and 4 more students join them. How many students are there in total?

________ + ________ = ________

There are _____ students in total.

4. In a zoo, 13 monkeys were swinging on a tree and 6 monkeys were playing on the ground. How many monkeys were there in all?

________ + ________ = ________

Thus, there were ________ monkeys in all.

4 Subtraction up to 20

Prior Knowledge

- Counting objects
- Counting backward

Learning Objectives

- Subtraction
- Subtract using backward counting
- Subtract using a number line
- Subtraction facts
- Subtraction of 1-digit number from 2-digit number
- Solving word problems of subtraction

Let's Get Started

Match the objects with their count.

1 less than 2	1 less than 4	1 less than 5	1 less than 3

INTRODUCTION TO SUBTRACTION

Bala has 7 umbrellas and he gives Benu 3 umbrellas. Let us find out the total number of umbrellas left with Bala.

3 umbrellas taken away from 7 leaves 4 umbrellas.

Taking away things to find out how much is left is called **subtraction**. We use the sign '–' to show subtraction.

This symbol '–' is read as **minus**.

So, 7 umbrellas – 3 umbrellas = 4 umbrellas.

It is read as 7 minus 3 is equal to 4.

It can also be shown vertically.

	O
	7
–	3
	4

EXERCISE 4.1

1. Cross and subtract the following.

a. 3 – 1 = ☐

b. 5 – 3 = ☐

c. 8 – 5 = ☐

d. 4 – 1 = ☐

e. 9 – 6 = ☐

2. Subtract the following.

a. 2 – 1 = ☐ b. 3 – 1 = ☐ c. 4 – 3 = ☐

d. 5 – 4 = ☐ e. 6 – 2 = ☐ f. 6 – 5 = ☐

g. 9 – 2 = ☐ h. 8 – 1 = ☐ i. 7 – 6 = ☐

3. Subtract the following.

a.	b.	c.	d.	e.
3	4	5	2	4
– 2	– 1	– 3	– 1	– 3

f.	g.	h.	i.	j.
3	6	7	8	9
– 0	– 2	– 4	– 3	– 1

k.	l.	m.	n.	o.
5	7	4	9	6
– 4	– 2	– 3	– 0	– 4

SUBTRACTION USING BACKWARD COUNTING

We can subract one number from the other by **counting backward**.

Let us subtract 5 from 9.

9 – 5 = 9 → 8 → 7 → 6 → 5 → 4

So, 9 – 5 = 4

SUBTRACTION FACTS

Fact 1: When we subtract 1 from a number, the answer is the number just before it.

Example 1: Solve 3 – 1 on the number line.

REMEMBER

To subtract on a number line, we always move to the left.

Solution: To subtract 1 from 3, we begin from 3 and move 1 place to the left. We reach 2.

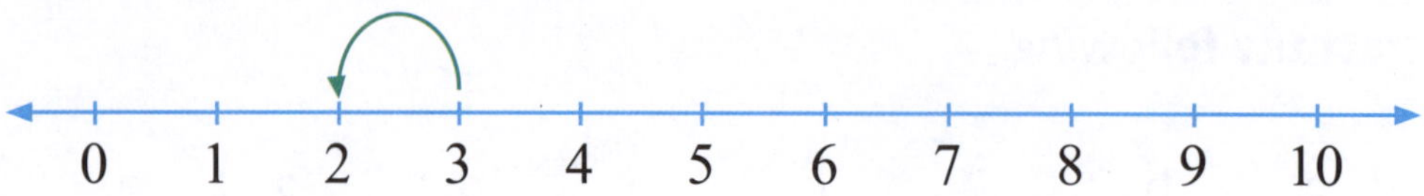

So, 3 – 1 = 2.

Fact 2: If 0 is subtracted from a number, the answer remains the same number. Its value does not decrease.

Example 2: Solve 7 – 0 on the number line.

Solution: We begin from 7 but do not move to the left. We stay at 7.

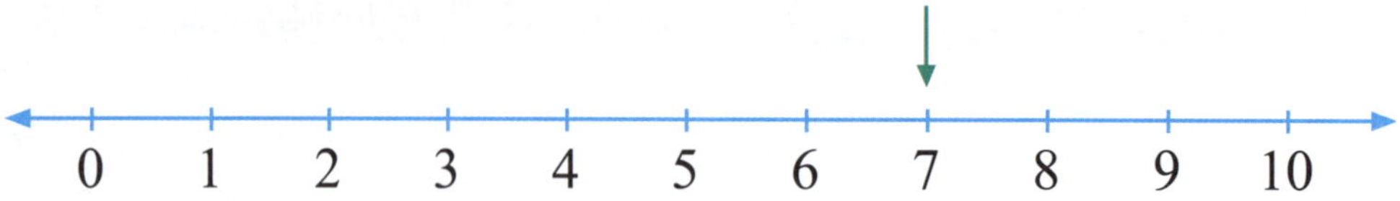

So, 7 – 0 = 7.

Fact 3: When you subtract a number from the same number, the answer is always 0.

Example 3: Ria gives all her 11 stickers to Mayank. How many stickers are left with Ria?

Solution: Take away 11 stickers from 11 stickers, we get

	T	O
	1	1
–	1	1
	0	0

So, Ria is left with 0 stickers.

Exercise 4.2

1. Subtract the following on the number line.

a. 6 – 2 = ______

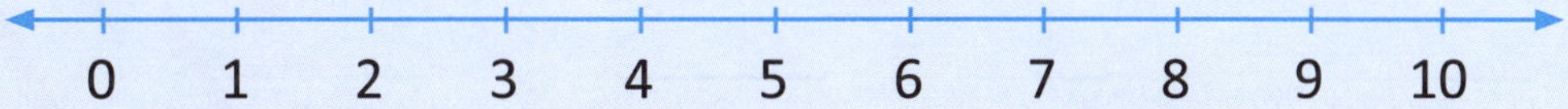

b. 5 – 3 = ______

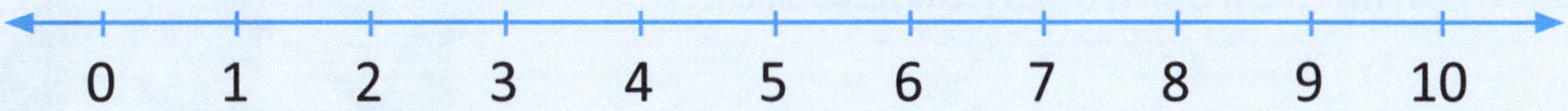

c. 7 – 4 = ______

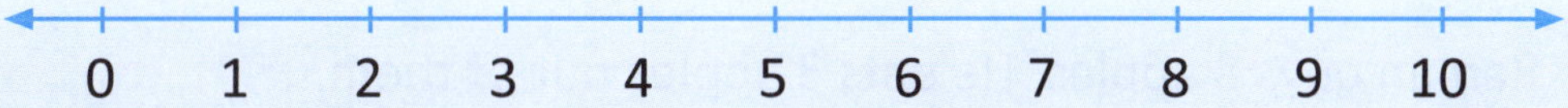

d. 19 – 0 = ______

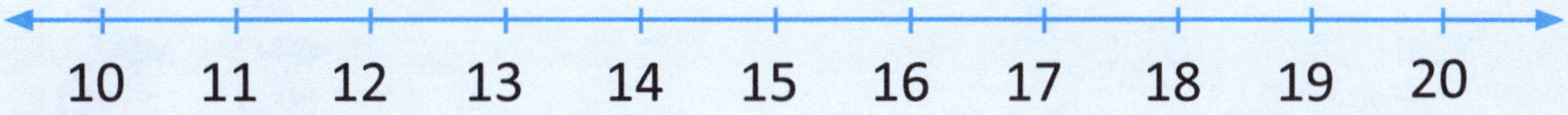

e. 15 – 3 = ______

2. Subtract the following.

a. 12 – 1 = ______ b. 10 – 0 = ______ c. 16 – 16 = ______

d. 15 – 0 = ______ e. 11 – 11 = ______ f. 9 – 1 = ______

WORD PROBLEMS

Example 4: Rita buys 5 ice creams.
She eats 3 ice creams out of them.
How many ice creams are left with Rita?

Solution: Out of 5 ice creams, Rita eats 3 ice creams.

5 – 3 = 2

Thus, 2 ice creams are left with Rita.

Remember

Whenever something reduces, we subtract.

EXERCISE 4.3

Solve the following word problems.

1. Sita has 5 pencils. She loses 2 pencils. How many pencils are left with her now?

_______ – _______ = _______

So, _______ pencils are left with Sita.

2. There are 4 birds sitting on a tree. 1 bird flies away. How many birds are left on the tree?

_______ – _______ = _______

There are _______ birds left on the tree.

3. Raman buys 8 apples. He eats 3 apples out of them. How many apples are left with Raman now?

_______ – _______ = _______

_______ apples are left with Raman.

4. In a garden, there are 6 trees. 4 trees fall down during a storm. How many trees are left in the garden?

_______ – _______ = _______

There are _______ trees left in the garden.

SUBTRACTION OF 1-DIGIT NUMBERS FROM 2-DIGIT NUMBERS

Example 5: Sneha buys 13 apples. Her brother eats 2 apples. How many apples are left?

Solution: 13 apples – 2 apples

	T	O
	1	3
–		2
	1	1

So, 13 apples – 2 apples = 11 apples.

Example 6: There are 15 kites flying in the sky. 10 kites fall down. How many kites were flying in the sky?

Solution: 15 kites – 10 kites

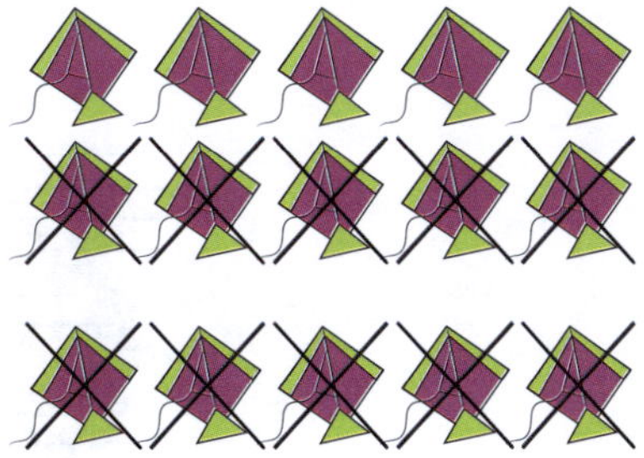

	T	O
	1	5
–	1	0
		5

So, 15 kites – 10 kites = 5 kites.

EXERCISE 4.4

1. Subtract the following.

a.

	T	O
	1	8
–		2

b.

	T	O
	1	7
–		5

c.

	T	O
	1	1
–		1

d.

	T	O
	1	9
–		7

e.

	T	O
	2	0
–		0

f.

	T	O
	1	5
–		3

g.

	T	O
	1	2
–		1

h.

	T	O
	1	6
–		4

i.

	T	O
	1	3
–		2

j.

	T	O
	1	4
–		2

k.

	T	O
	1	8
–		7

l.

	T	O
	1	7
–		4

2. **Arhaan has 19 coins. He gives 3 coins to his friend. How many coins are left with him now?**

	T	O
–		

☐ coins are left with Arhaan.

3. **There are 18 cars in the school car park. 12 cars drive away. How many cars are left in the school car park?**

	T	O
–		

☐ cars are left in the school car park.

4. **There are 20 birds sitting on a tree. 10 birds flew away. How many birds are left now?**

	T	O
–		

☐ birds are left now.

Key Concepts

Subtraction up to 20

- **Subtraction with single digits**

  Subtract 6 – 3.
  Counting backward
  6, 5, 4, 3
  Therefore, 6 – 3 = 3.

- **Subtracting 0 from a number**

  6 – 0 = 6

- **Subtracting a number from itself**

  6 – 6 = 0

- **Subtraction of 1-digit numbers from 2-digit numbers**

  Subtract 18 – 6.
  Arrange the numbers according to their place value.
  Subtract the ones, that is, 8 – 6 = 2.
  Subtract the tens, that is, 1 – 0 = 1.
  Therefore, 18 – 6 = 12.

	T	O
	1	8
–		6
	1	2

Revision Exercise

1. Choose the correct option.

a. 6 – 2 = ________

i. 8 ii. 6 iii. 4 iv. 2

b. 7 – 4 = ________

i. 9 ii. 7 iii. 5 iv. 3

c. 8 – 0 = ________

i. 0 ii. 8 iii. 7 iv. 6

d. 14 – 1 = ________

i. 11 ii. 12 iii. 13 iv. 14

2. Subtract the following.

a.

	O
	5
–	0

b.

	T	O
	1	7
–		2

c.

	T	O
	1	9
–	1	3

d.

	T	O
	1	8
–		8

3. Subtract using the number line.

a. 7 – 2 = __________

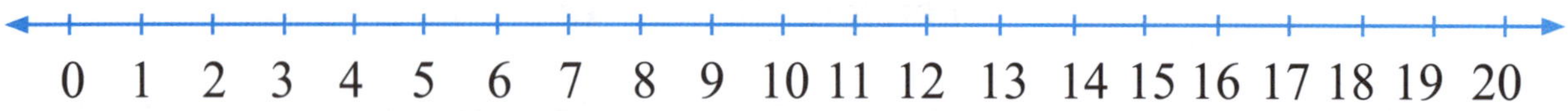

b. 19 – 5 = __________

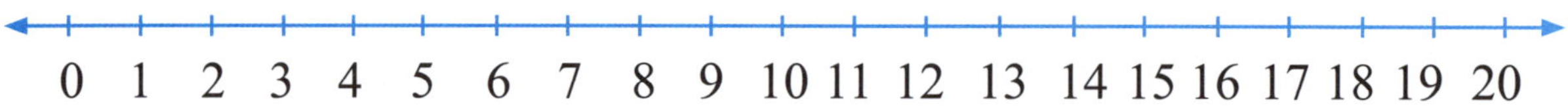

4. Rahim has 19 marbles. He loses 9 marbles out of them. How many marbles does Rahim have now?

	T	O
–		

Rahim has ☐ marbles with him now.

5. **Pooja has 15 flowers in her garden. She plucks 4 flowers. How many flowers are left in her garden?**

	T	O
−		

There are ☐ flowers left in Pooja's garden.

6. **There were 13 books on a shelf. Savita gives away 11 books to her friends. How many books are left on the shelf?**

	T	O
−		

There are ☐ books left on the shelf.

7. **Udoy buys 11 ice cream cones. He and his friends ate 3 eat creams. How many ice creams cones are left?**

	T	O
−		

☐ ice creams cones are left.

5 Addition up to 99

Prior Knowledge

- Addition up to 20
- Horizontal addition
- Vertical addition

Learning Objectives

- Adding tens
- Adding 2-digit numbers with or without regrouping
- Addition of two 3-digit numbers without regrouping
- Solving word problems of addition

Let's Get Started

Help the monkey to get the bananas. Add the numbers and write the answer in the given circles.

ADDITION BY TENS

Let us add 20 and 10.

There are 0 ones. So, add the tens only.

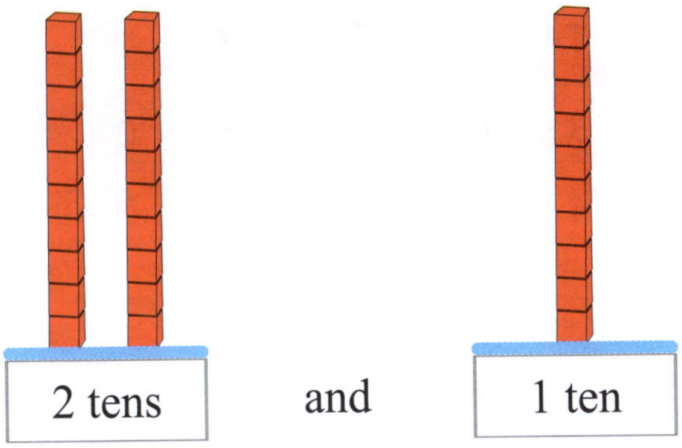

	T	O
	2	0
+	1	0
	3	0

So, $20 + 10 = 30$.

Example 1: Add 27 and 10.

Solution: Add the **ones**.

7 ones + 0 ones = 7 ones

	T	O
	2	7
+	1	0
		7

Add the **tens**.

2 tens + 1 ten = 3 tens

	T	O
	2	7
+	1	0
	3	7

So, $27 + 10 = 37$

We can solve addition sums mentally.

Example 2: Find $23 + 10$.

Solution: Regroup 23 into tens and ones. $23 = 20 + 3$

Add the tens. $20 + 10 = 30$

Add the result to the ones. $3 + 30 = 33$

So, $23 + 10 = 33$.

Exercise 5.1

Find the sums.

1.

	T	O
	3	0
+	1	0

2.

	T	O
	4	0
+	2	0

3.

	T	O
	3	0
+	4	0

4.

	T	O
	5	0
+	3	0

5.

	T	O
	3	2
+	2	0

6.

	T	O
	4	5
+	1	0

7.

	T	O
	5	7
+	3	0

8.

	T	O
	4	0
+	2	8

9.

	T	O
	6	5
+	3	0

10.

	T	O
	8	5
+	1	0

11.

	T	O
	2	8
+	4	0

12.

	T	O
	3	9
+	5	0

ADDITION OF 1- AND 2-DIGIT NUMBERS WITHOUT REGROUPING

Example 3: Add 42 and 5.

Solution:

	Add the tens	Add the ones
	4 tens	2 ones
+		5 ones
	4 tens	7 ones

	T	O
	4	2
+		5
	4	7

Hence, 42 + 5 = 47.

Remember

Always write the tens digit below the tens place and the ones digit below the ones place.

EXERCISE 5.2

Add the following numbers.

1.

	T	O
	3	2
+		4

2.

	T	O
	8	2
+		6

3.

	T	O
	5	7
+		2

4.

	T	O
	4	6
+		3

5.

	T	O
	1	5
+		3

6.

	T	O
	2	4
+		5

7.

	T	O
	6	1
+		8

8.

	T	O
	3	9
+		0

9.

	T	O
	6	5
+		2

10.

	T	O
	8	1
+		5

11.

	T	O
	7	2
+		4

12.

	T	O
	9	2
+		5

ADDITION OF TWO 2-DIGIT NUMBERS WITHOUT REGROUPING

Example 4: Add 73 and 14.

Solution:

	Add the tens	Add the ones
	7 tens	3 ones
+	1 ten	4 ones
	8 tens	7 ones

	T	O
	7	3
+	1	4
	8	7

Hence, 73 + 14 = 87.

EXERCISE 5.3

Add the following numbers.

1.

	T	O
	4	7
+	3	1

2.

	T	O
	7	1
+	2	6

3.

	T	O
	8	2
+	1	7

4.

	T	O
	1	2
+	3	4

5.

	T	O
	4	4
+	2	1

6.

	T	O
	7	8
+	1	0

7.

	T	O
	5	5
+	2	2

8.

	T	O
	1	2
+	3	3

9.

	T	O
	5	0
+	2	0

10.

	T	O
	7	4
+	2	5

11.

	T	O
	7	2
+	2	6

12.

	T	O
	8	0
+	1	5

ADDITION OF THREE 2-DIGIT NUMBERS WITHOUT REGROUPING

Example 5: Solve 23 + 14 + 31.

Solution: First add the digits in the ones column, that is, 3 + 4 + 1 = 8. Then, add the digits in the tens column, that is, 2 + 1 + 3 = 6.

So, 23 + 14 + 31 = 68.

	T	O
	2	3
	1	4
+	3	1
	6	8

Exercise 5.4

Add the following numbers.

1.

	T	O
	3	4
+	2	1
	1	3

2.

	T	O
	6	2
+	1	0
	2	7

3.

	T	O
	7	4
+	1	0
	1	3

4.

	T	O
	2	3
+	1	4
	5	1

5.

	T	O
	4	5
+	2	3
	3	0

6.

	T	O
	5	0
+	2	7
	1	0

7.

	T	O
	2	3
+	1	4
	3	1

8.

	T	O
	4	1
+	1	3
	1	5

ADDITION OF 2-DIGIT AND 1-DIGIT NUMBERS WITH REGROUPING

Let us add 28 and 7 by regrouping ones.

	T	O
	2	8
+		7

Step 1: Add the ones, that is, 8 ones + 7 ones = 15 ones = 1 ten 5 ones

	T	O
	[1]2	8
+		7
		5

Step 2: Carry over 1 ten from ones place to tens place and write 5 in the ones place.

	T	O
	[1]2	8
+		7
	3	5

Step 3: Now adding the carried over 1 ten to the 2 tens, we get 3 tens.
Write 3 in the tens place.

So, 28 + 7 = 35.

Let us now add 37 and 6 using an abacus.

First add the beads on the ones rod. Then, add the beads on the tens rod.

> **REMEMBER**
> Addition with regrouping is also called carry over.

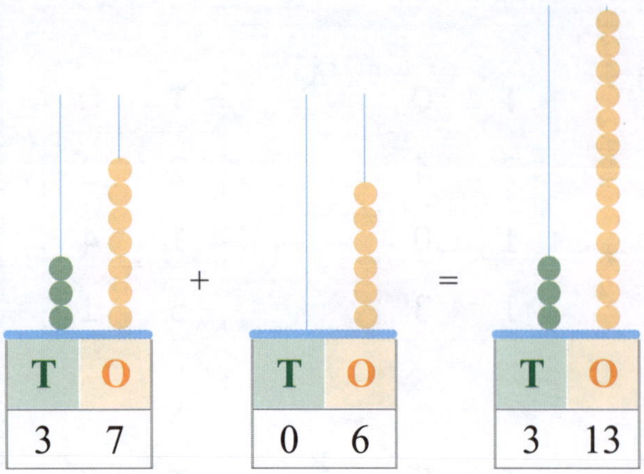

or

3 tens	+	7 ones
0 tens	+	6 ones
3 tens	+	13 ones

So, 3 tens + 13 ones

= 3 tens + 1 ten + 3 ones

= 4 tens + 3 ones

= 40 + 3 = 43

Therefore, 37 + 6 = 43.

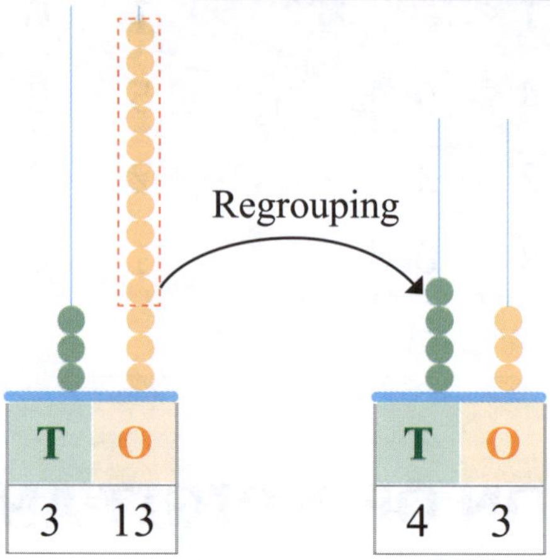

ADDITION OF TWO 2-DIGIT NUMBERS WITH REGROUPING

Example 6: Add 25 and 37.

Solution: Step 1: Add the ones.

5 ones + 7 ones = 12 ones

12 ones = 1 ten 2 ones

Write 2 in the ones column and carry over 1 ten to the tens column.

	T	O
	[1] 2	5
+	3	7
		2

Step 2: Add the tens.

1 ten + 2 tens + 3 tens

= 6 tens

Write 6 tens in the tens column.

So, 25 + 37 = 62.

	T	O
	[1] 2	5
+	3	7
	6	2

Exercise 5.5

Add the following numbers.

1.

	T	O
	7	7
+		6

2.

	T	O
	6	2
+		8

3.

	T	O
	4	3
+		9

4.

	T	O
	5	9
+		3

5.

	T	O
	8	8
+		2

6.

	T	O
	4	8
+		4

7.

	T	O
	7	4
+		6

8.

	T	O
	5	4
+		7

9.

	T	O
	6	2
+	1	9

10.

	T	O
	3	7
+	4	5

11.

	T	O
	5	1
+	2	9

12.

	T	O
	3	4
+	5	8

13.

	T	O
	5	6
+	3	8

14.

	T	O
	7	3
+	1	9

15.

	T	O
	3	2
+	5	9

16.

	T	O
	4	9
+	2	7

17.

	T	O
	6	5
+	1	8

18.

	T	O
	5	7
+	3	6

19.

	T	O
	4	2
+	4	9

20.

	T	O
	5	2
+	2	9

ADDITION OF TWO 3-DIGIT NUMBERS

Let us add 136 and 321.

Step 1: Add the **ones**.

6 ones + 1 one = 7 ones

	H	T	O
	1	3	6
+	3	2	1
			7

Step 2: Add the **tens**.

3 tens + 2 tens = 5 tens

	H	T	O
	1	3	6
+	3	2	1
		5	7

Step 3: Add the **hundreds**.

1 hundred + 3 hundreds = 4 hundreds

	H	T	O
	1	3	6
+	3	2	1
	4	5	7

Thus, 136 + 321 = 457.

Find the sums.

1.

	H	T	O
	1	3	5
+	2	4	2

2.

	H	T	O
	3	2	4
+	3	4	5

3.

	H	T	O
	2	4	3
+	1	2	4

4.

	H	T	O
	1	5	6
+	4	2	3

5.

	H	T	O
	2	3	3
+	2	4	5

6.

	H	T	O
	5	2	5
+	1	3	2

7.

	H	T	O
	4	1	2
+	2	3	7

8.

	H	T	O
	3	6	3
+	2	1	5

9.

	H	T	O
	2	3	4
+	3	4	1

WORD PROBLEMS

Example 7: An ice cream vendor sold 45 ice creams on Monday and 32 ice creams on Tuesday. How many ice creams did he sell on these two days?

Solution:

Number of ice creams sold on Monday = 45

Number of ice creams sold on Tuesday = 32

Total ice creams sold = 45 + 32 = 77

Thus, the ice cream vendor sold 77 ice creams on these two days.

	T	O
	4	5
+	3	2
	7	7

Example 8: There are 23 purple flowers and 8 yellow flowers in the garden. What is the total number of flowers in the garden?

Solution:

Number of purple flowers = 23

Number of yellow flowers = 8

Total number of flowers = 23 + 8 = 31

Thus, there are 31 flowers in the garden.

	T	O
	[1]2	3
+		8
	3	1

EXERCISE 5.6

Solve the following word problems on addition.

1. For a picnic, children carried 12 bottles of orange juice and 6 bottles of guava juice. How many bottles of juice did the children carry?

   Number of bottles of orange juice = ☐

   Number of bottles of guava juice = ☐

   Total number of bottles of juice = ☐

   Thus, children carried ☐ bottles of juice.

	T	O
+		

2. Sam read 34 pages of a storybook on Saturday and 6 pages on Sunday. How many pages did he read on these two days?

   Number of pages read on Saturday = ☐

   Number of pages read on Sunday = ☐

   Total number of pages read = ☐

   Thus, Sam read ☐ number of pages on these two days.

	T	O
+		

3. At the school car park, there are 53 red cars and 25 green cars. What is the total number of cars parked?

Number of red cars parked = ☐

Number of green cars parked = ☐

Total number of cars parked = ☐

Thus, there are ☐ cars parked.

	T	O
+		

4. Class 1 has 12 students, Class 2 has 14 students and Class 3 has 11 students. How many total students are there in these classes?

Number of students in Class 1 = ☐

Number of students in Class 2 = ☐

Number of students in Class 3 = ☐

Total number of students = ☐

Thus, there are ☐ students in these classes.

	T	O
+		

5. In a school, 67 students like to play cricket and 25 students like to play volleyball. How many students like to play cricket and volleyball?

Number of students who like to play cricket = ☐

Number of students who like to play volleyball = ☐

Total number of students = ☐

Thus, ☐ students like to play cricket and volleyball.

	T	O
+		

6. 22 students like painting, 24 children like dancing and 11 students like swimming. How many students like painting, dancing and swimming in total?

Number of students who like painting = ☐

Number of students who like dancing = ☐

Number of students who like swimming = ☐

Total number of students = ☐

Thus, ☐ students like painting, dancing and swimming.

	T	O
+		

KEY CONCEPTS

Addition up to 99

Adding tens

40 + 10 = 50

Step 1: Add ones.

Step 2: Add the tens.

	T	O
	4	0
+	1	0
	5	0

Addition of 2-digit and 1-digit numbers

Step 1: Add the ones.

Step 2: Add the tens.

	T	O
	2	6
+		3
	2	9

Adding two 2-digit numbers

Step 1: Add the ones.

Step 2: Add the tens.

	T	O
	2	6
+	1	3
	3	9

Adding three numbers

Step 1: Add the ones.

Step 2: Add the tens.

	T	O
	1	2
	2	3
+	1	4
	4	9

Addition of two 3-digit numbers

Step 1: Add the ones.

Step 2: Add the tens.

Step3 : Add the hundreds.

	H	T	O
	3	6	3
+	2	1	5
	5	7	8

Revision Exercise

1. Match the questions in columns A and C to their answers in column B.

A

	T	O
	1	2
	2	3
+	4	1

	T	O
	6	3
+		4

	T	O
	4	2
+	1	3

B

67

568

55

76

43

60

C

	T	O
	3	9
+		4

	T	O
	4	0
+	2	0

	H	T	O
	2	0	5
+	3	6	3

2. Add mentally.

a. 35 + 10 = ______ b. 20 + 27 = ______

c. 15 + ______ = 45 d. 17 + ______ = 27

e. 19 + 30 = ______ f. 24 + ______ = 64

g. 152 + 100 = ______ h. 139 + 200 = ______

3. Add the following numbers on the abacus by drawing beads.

a. 43 + 5

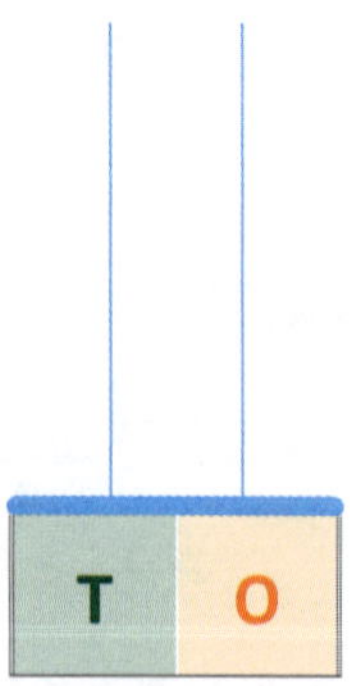

b. 70 + 9

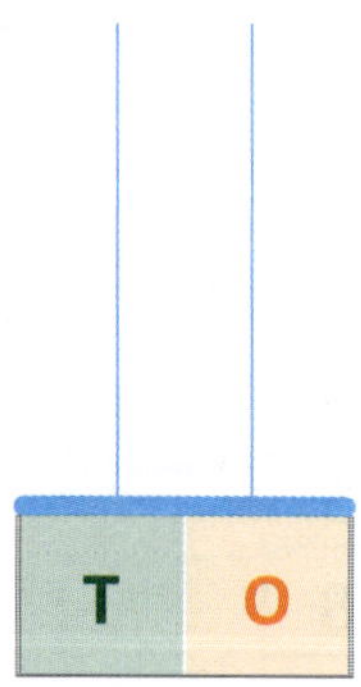

4. Sanjana was drawing a scenery for her drawing competition. She drew 16 trees and 10 flowers. How many trees and flowers did she draw in total?

	T	O
+		

5. Amanpreet spent ₹45 for buying one storybook and Siya spent ₹34 to buy a comic book. How much did they spend in all?

	T	O
+		

6. Priya's mother gave her 28 cookies one day and 15 cookies another day. How many cookies did her mother give Priya in all?

	T	O
+		

7. In a movie hall, there were 50 men, 29 women and 10 children. How many people were there in the movie hall?

	T	O
+		

6 Subtraction up to 99

Prior Knowledge

- Meaning of addition and subtraction
- Taking away to subtract
- Counting back to subtract
- Subtracting 2-digit numbers

Learning Objectives

- Subtracting tens
- Subtracting 1-digit numbers from 2-digit numbers using various techniques
- Subtracting 2-digit numbers with or without regrouping
- Solving word problems on subtraction

Let's Get Started

Colour the picture according to the given code.

= 11

= 12

= 13

= 14

= 15

= 17

= 20

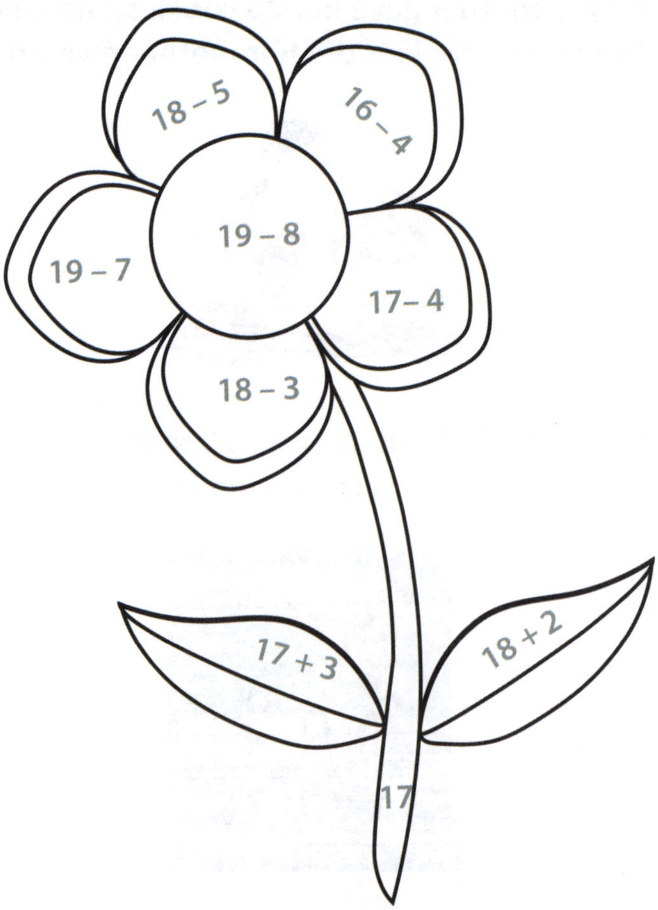

SUBTRACTING TENS

Let us subtract 10, 20, 30, ... from a 2-digit number.

Example 1: Subtract 20 from 50.

Solution: To subtract 20 from 50, we write the numbers in respective columns as—

	T	O
	5	0
–	2	0
	3	0

Step 1: Subtract the ones. 0 – 0 = 0

Step 2: Subtract the tens. 5 – 2 = 3

So, 50 – 20 = 30.

EXERCISE 6.1

Find the difference.

1.

	T	O
	4	0
–	1	0

2.

	T	O
	6	0
–	3	0

3.

	T	O
	5	0
–	4	0

4.

	T	O
	7	0
–	3	0

5.

	T	O
	2	6
–	1	0

6.

	T	O
	4	5
–	2	0

7.

	T	O
	4	8
–	3	0

8.

	T	O
	5	7
–	2	0

SUBTRACTION OF 1-DIGIT AND 2-DIGIT NUMBERS FROM 2-DIGIT NUMBERS WITHOUT REGROUPING

Example 2: Solve 68 – 6.

Solution:

	Subtract the tens	Subtract the ones
	6 tens	8 ones
–		6 ones
	6 tens	2 ones

	T	O
	6	8
–		6
	6	2

Hence, 68 – 6 = 62.

Let us now subtract 6 from 68 using an abacus.

Show the number 68 on the abacus.

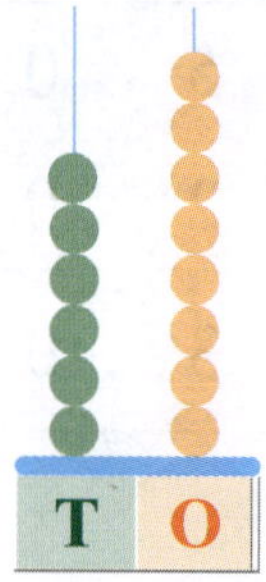

Take 6 beads away from the ones rod and read the new number formed from the remaining beads.

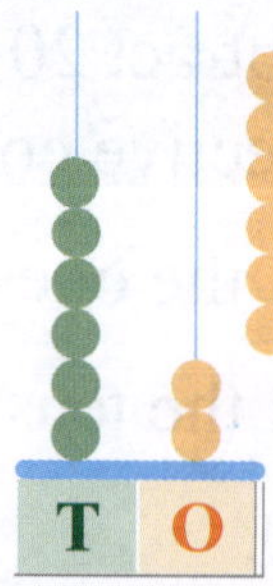

6 tens and 2 ones

Hence, 68 – 6 = 62.

Example 3: Solve 47 – 35.

Solution:

	Subtract the tens	Subtract the ones
	4 tens	7 ones
–	3 tens	5 ones
	1 tens	2 ones

	T	O
	4	7
–	3	5
	1	2

Hence, 47 – 35 = 12.

Exercise 6.2

Subtract the following.

1.

	T	O
	5	6
–	2	4

2.

	T	O
	7	5
–	3	1

3.

	T	O
	6	7
–	1	5

4.

	T	O
	4	7
–	3	2

5.

	T	O
	4	9
–	2	7

6.

	T	O
	4	8
–	1	6

7.

	T	O
	7	5
–	3	4

8.

	T	O
	9	8
–	3	7

9.

	T	O
	3	9
−	2	8

10.

	T	O
	7	8
−	4	6

11.

	T	O
	8	2
−	1	2

12.

	T	O
	6	8
−	3	7

SUBTRACTION OF 1-DIGIT AND 2-DIGIT NUMBERS FROM 2-DIGIT NUMBERS WITH REGROUPING

Example 4: Solve 36 – 9.

Solution: **Step 1:** We cannot take away 9 ones from 6 ones.

So, we use regrouping.

Regroup the tens and the ones in 36.

36 = 3 tens + 6 ones

= 2 tens + 16 ones

	T	O
	$^{2}\cancel{3}$	$^{16}\cancel{6}$
–		9
		7

Step 2: Subtract the ones.

16 ones – 9 ones = 7 ones

Step 3: Subtract the tens.

2 tens – 0 tens = 2 tens

Hence, 36 – 9 = 27.

	T	O
	$^{2}\cancel{3}$	$^{16}\cancel{6}$
–		9
	2	7

Example 5: Subtract 36 from 52.

Solution:

Since 2 < 6, regroup 52 into tens and ones.

	T	O
	5	2
–	3	6

→

Subtract the ones. 12 – 6 = 6

	T	O
	$^{4}\cancel{5}$	$^{12}\cancel{2}$
–	3	6
		6

→

Subtract the tens. 4 – 3 = 1

	T	O
	$^{4}\cancel{5}$	$^{12}\cancel{2}$
–	3	6
	1	6

Hence, 52 – 36 = 16.

Exercise 6.3

Subtract the following.

1.

	T	O
	8	2
–		5

2.

	T	O
	7	9
–		9

3.

	T	O
	5	3
–		7

4.

	T	O
	3	8
–		9

5.

	T	O
	4	8
–		9

6.

	T	O
	2	5
–		6

7.

	T	O
	9	0
–		8

8.

	T	O
	4	4
–		9

9.

	T	O
	4	3
–	1	9

10.

	T	O
	5	6
–	2	8

11.

	T	O
	2	7
–	1	9

12.

	T	O
	3	7
–	2	8

13.

	T	O
	6	4
–	2	7

14.

	T	O
	7	5
–	3	8

15.

	T	O
	9	2
–	6	4

16.

	T	O
	4	8
–	3	9

WORD PROBLEMS

If the quantity of any object gets reduced, we perform subtraction to find out how much is left.

Example 6: Out of 39 students in a class, 17 students are absent. How many students are present in the class?

Solution: Total students in the class = 39

Number of students absent = 17

Number of students present = 39 – 17 = 22

Thus, 22 students are present in the class.

	T	O
	3	9
–	1	7
	2	2

Example 7: Out of 12 apples, Ramesh ate 3. How many apples were left?

Solution: Total number of apples = 12

Number of apples Ramesh ate = 3

Number of apples left = 12 – 3 = 9

Thus, 9 apples were left.

	T	O
	0 ~~1~~	12 ~~2~~
–		3
		9

EXERCISE 6.4

1. Out of 57 pages in a book, Rajesh read 7 pages. How many pages were left to be read?

Total number of pages = ☐

Number of pages read = ☐

Number of pages left = ☐

Thus, ☐ pages were left to be read.

	T	O
–		

2. Out of 95 ice creams, an ice cream vendor sold 64 ice creams in one day. How many ice creams were left with him?

Total number of ice creams = ☐

Number of ice creams sold = ☐

Number of ice creams left = ☐

Thus, ☐ ice creams were left with the vendor.

	T	O
–		

3. Out of 89 flowers in a garden, 39 are roses. How many flowers are not roses?

Total number of flowers = ☐

Number of roses = ☐

Number of flowers that are not roses = ☐

Thus, ☐ flowers are not roses.

	T	O
–		

4. In a park, there are 55 children, out of which 24 are boys. How many girls were there?

Total number of children = ☐

Number of boys = ☐

Number of girls = ☐

Thus, there were ☐ girls.

	T	O
–		

5. **An orchard has 93 trees, out of which 9 are mango trees. How many trees are not mango trees?**

Total number of trees = ☐

Number of mango trees = ☐

Number of trees that are not mango trees = ☐

Thus, ☐ trees are not mango trees.

	T	O
–		

KEY CONCEPTS

Subtraction up to 99

Subtracting tens

40 – 30

Step 1: Subtract the ones.

Step 2: Subtract the tens.

	T	O
	4	0
–	3	0
	1	**0**

Subtraction of 1-digit number from 2-digit number

25 – 2

Step 1: Subtract the ones.

Step 2: Subtract the tens.

	T	O
	2	5
–		2
	2	**3**

Subtraction of 2-digit number from 2-digit number

26 – 13

Step 1: Subtract the ones.

Step 2: Subtract the tens.

	T	O
	2	6
–	1	3
	1	**3**

Revision Exercise

1. Circle the correct answer.

a. 50 – 30 = ________

10	20	40

b. 80 – 20 = ________

40	50	60

c. 45 – 30 = ________

15	30	45

d. 65 – 15 = ________

50	60	70

2. Match the questions in row A to their answers in row B.

A.

	T	O
	9	7
–	4	6

	T	O
	5	6
–		8

	T	O
	7	9
–	5	4

	T	O
	2	8
–	1	5

B. 25 13 51 48

3. Solve the word problems.

a. Out of 34 children in a class, 5 do not like to play cricket. How many children like to play cricket?

b. Out of 25 birds sitting on a tree, 8 birds fly away. How many birds are left?

c. There are 56 mangoes in a basket. Out of these 11 mangoes were rotten. How many fresh mangoes are there in the basket?

d. In a movie hall, there are 93 seats. 17 seats are occupied. How many seats are not occupied?

7 Introduction to Multiplication

Prior Knowledge

- Counting numbers in groups
- Concept of addition

Learning Objectives

- Representing repeated addition as multiplication
- Skip counting by 2s, 5s, and 10s
- Applying the multiplication tables
- Vertical multiplication
- Multiplication of 2-digit numbers

Let's Get Started

Add the objects and colour the answer in the given boxes.

1. 

7
6
8

2. 

19
18
17

3. 

9
8
7

4. 

14
15
16

5. 

14
15
16

6. 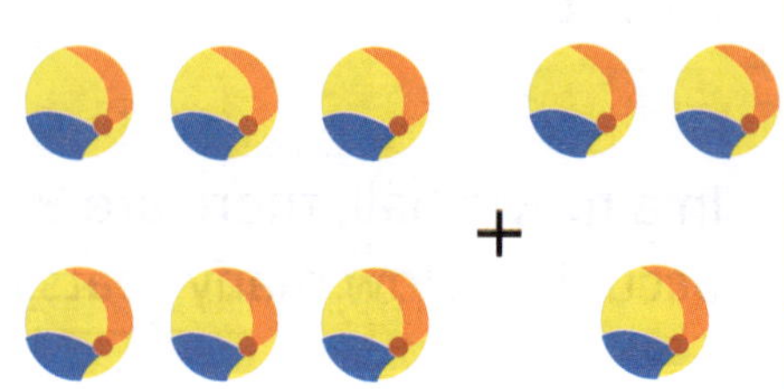

9
10
11

ADDING EQUAL GROUPS

Count the number of leaves.

There are 4 groups. There are 3 leaves in each group.

$3 + 3 + 3 + 3 = 12$ or 4 groups of $3 = 12$

So, there are 12 leaves in all.

Counting in equal groups is called **repeated addition**.

EXERCISE 7.1

Count the objects and fill in the blanks.

1. There are ______ groups of crayons.

   ______ + ______ = ______

   ______ groups of ______ = ______

2. There are ______ groups of inkpots.

   ______ + ______ + ______ + ______ = ______

   ______ groups of ______ = ______

3. There are ______ groups of sketch pens.

   ______ + ______ + ______ = ______

   ______ groups of ______ = ______

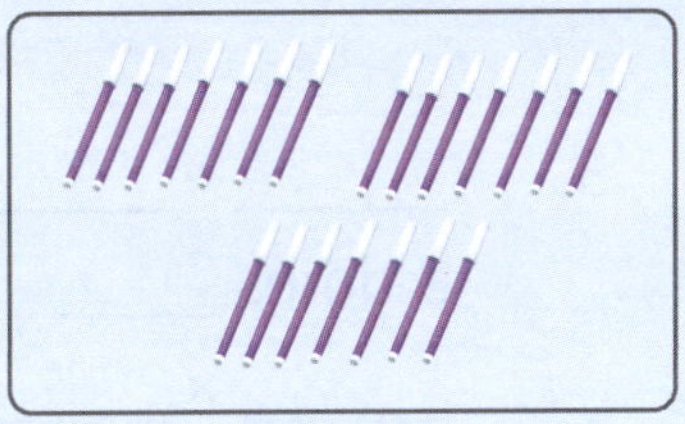

4. There are ______ groups of pinwheels.

   ______ + ______ = ______

   ______ groups of ______ = ______

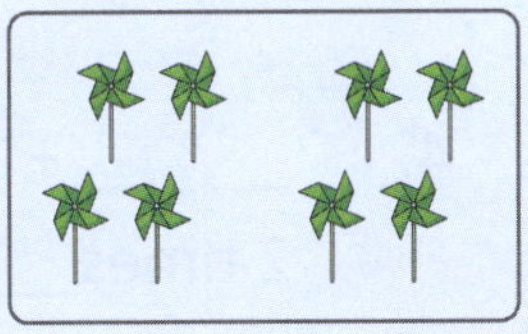

5. There are ______ groups of paint brushes.

   ______ + ______ + ______ + ______ + ______ = ______

   ______ groups of ______ = ______

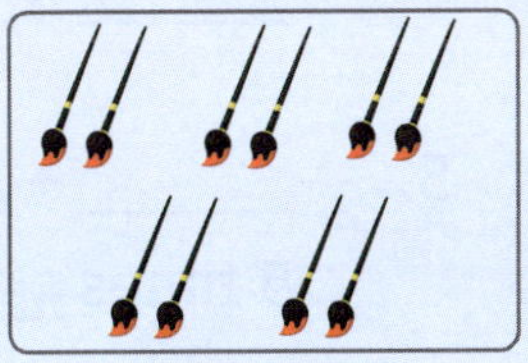

MULTIPLICATION AS REPEATED ADDITION

There are 2 boxes of eggs. There are 4 eggs in each box.

4 eggs + 4 eggs = 8 eggs

Or 2 **times** 4 = 8

Or 2 × 4 = 8

It is read as **two times four is equal to eight**.

REMEMBER

× is read as **times**. It is the symbol for **multiplication.**

EXERCISE 7.2

Fill in the missing numbers. One has been done for you.

1. __2__ + __2__ + __2__ = __6__
   3 times __2__ = __6__
   __3__ × __2__ = __6__

2. ______ + ______ + ______ + ______ = ______
   4 times ______ = ______
   ______ × ______ = ______

3. ______ + ______ + ______ = ______
   3 times ______ = ______
   ______ × ______ = ______

4. ______ + ______ = ______
   2 times ______ = ______
   ______ × ______ = ______

5. ______ + ______ + ______ + ______ + ______ = ______
   5 times ______ = ______
   ______ × ______ = ______

SKIP COUNTING

Let's start counting from 2 leaving a number in between.

1	2	3	4	5	6	7	8	9	10
11	12	13	14	15	16	17	18	19	20

This is called **counting by 2s** as we count every second number.

Write down the pattern obtained.

2

Cross out the numbers, starting from 5 and leaving the next 4 numbers in between.

1	2	3	4	5	6	7	8	9	10
11	12	13	14	15	16	17	18	19	20
21	22	23	24	25	26	27	28	29	30

This is **counting by 5s**, as we count every fifth number.

Write down the pattern obtained.

5

Counting by 10s, colour the correct number box.

1	2	3	4	5	6	7	8	9	10
11	12	13	14	15	16	17	18	19	20
21	22	23	24	25	26	27	28	29	30
31	32	33	34	35	36	37	38	39	40
41	42	43	44	45	46	47	48	49	50

This is **counting by 10s**, as we count every tenth number.

Write down the pattern obtained.

10

MULTIPLICATION TABLES

Count and write the multiplication table of 1.

$1 \times 1 = 1$

$2 \times 1 = 2$

$3 \times 1 = \square$

$4 \times 1 = \square$

$5 \times 1 = \square$

$6 \times 1 = \square$

$7 \times 1 = \square$

$8 \times 1 = \square$

$9 \times 1 = \square$

$10 \times 1 = \square$

Count and write the multiplication table of 2.

$1 \times 2 = 2$

$2 \times 2 = 4$

$3 \times 2 = \square$

$4 \times 2 = \square$

$5 \times 2 = \square$

$6 \times 2 = \square$

$7 \times 2 = \square$

$8 \times 2 = \square$

$9 \times 2 = \square$

$10 \times 2 = \square$

Count and write the multiplication table of 3.

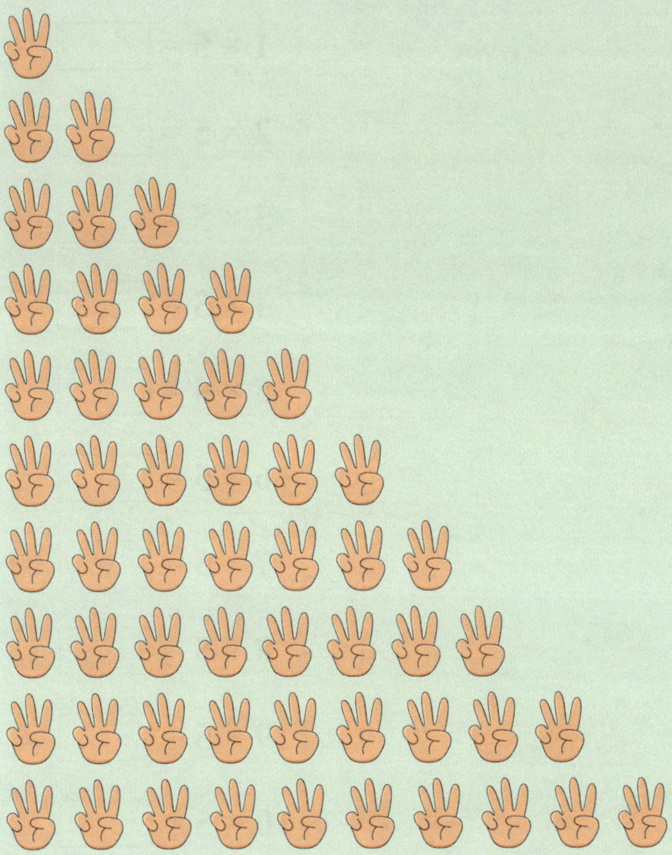

$1 \times 3 = \square$

$2 \times 3 = \square$

$3 \times 3 = \square$

$4 \times 3 = \square$

$5 \times 3 = \square$

$6 \times 3 = \square$

$7 \times 3 = \square$

$8 \times 3 = \square$

$9 \times 3 = \square$

$10 \times 3 = \square$

Count and write the multiplication table of 4.

$1 \times 4 = \square$

$2 \times 4 = \square$

$3 \times 4 = \square$

$4 \times 4 = \square$

$5 \times 4 = \square$

$6 \times 4 = \square$

$7 \times 4 = \square$

$8 \times 4 = \square$

$9 \times 4 = \square$

$10 \times 4 = \square$

Count and write the multiplication table of 5.

1 × 5 =

2 × 5 =

3 × 5 =

4 × 5 =

5 × 5 =

6 × 5 =

7 × 5 =

8 × 5 =

9 × 5 =

10 × 5 =

Count and write the multiplication table of 10.

1 × 10 =

2 × 10 =

3 × 10 =

4 × 10 =

5 × 10 =

6 × 10 =

7 × 10 =

8 × 10 =

9 × 10 =

10 × 10 =

EXERCISE 7.3

1. **Fill in the boxes with the help of the multiplication tables.**

a.	3 fours = 12 3 × 4 = 12	b. 2 fives = ______ 2 × 5 = ______	c. 5 twos = ______ 5 × 2 = ______
d.	1 twos = ______ 1 × 2 = ______	e. 3 threes = ______ 3 × 3 = ______	f. 2 tens = ______ 2 × 10 = ______
g.	7 threes = ______ 7 × 3 = ______	h. 9 fours = ______ 9 × 4 = ______	i. 6 ones = ______ 6 × 1 = ______

2. **Fill in the circles with the help of the multiplication tables.**

a. 3 × 2 = ◯ b. 4 × 3 = ◯ c. 2 × 4 = ◯

d. 7 × 5 = ◯ e. 6 × 3 = ◯ f. 4 × 4 = ◯

g. 3 × ◯ = 15 h. 7 × ◯ = 14 i. 6 × ◯ = 30

j. 9 × ◯ = 36 k. 8 × ◯ = 24 l. 5 × ◯ = 10

3. **Multiply the following numbers vertically. One has been done for you.**

a.

	O
	2
×	4
	8

b.

	O
	3
×	3

c.

	O
	4
×	2

d.

	O
	5
×	1

e.

	T	O
		3
×		5

f.

	T	O
		2
×		6

g.

	T	O
		5
×		4

h.

	T	O
		4
×		8

MULTIPLY 2-DIGIT NUMBERS BY 1-DIGIT NUMBERS

Sanya has 3 toffees in each box. If she has 11 boxes, let's find the number of toffees she has.

To find the total number of toffees, we multiply 11 by 3. Follow these steps.

Step 1: Write the number in their correct places.

	T	O
	1	1
×		3

Step 2: Multiply 1 at ones place by 3. We get 3.

	T	O
	1	1
×		3
		3

Step 3: Multiply 1 at tens place by 3. Again, we get 3.

	T	O
	1	1
×		3
	3	**3**

So, 11 times 3 = 11 × 3 = 33.

Exercise 7.4

Multiply.

1.

	T	O
	2	1
×		1

2.

	T	O
	2	4
×		2

3.

	T	O
	3	3
×		3

4.

	T	O
	3	1
×		1

5.

	T	O
	3	4
×		2

6.

	T	O
	4	2
×		2

Key Concepts

Introduction to multiplication

Adding equal groups → Repeated addition as multiplication

2 + 2 + 2 means 3 times 2.
2 + 2 + 2 = 6
3 × 2 = 6

Times tables of 1, 2, 3, 4, 5 and 10

×	1	2	3	4	5	10
1	1	2	3	4	5	10
2	2	4	6	8	10	20
3	3	6	9	12	15	30
4	4	8	12	16	20	40
5	5	10	15	20	25	50
6	6	12	18	24	30	60
7	7	14	21	28	35	70
8	8	16	24	32	40	80
9	9	18	27	36	45	90
10	10	20	30	40	50	100

Vertical multiplication

	T	O
	3	4
×		2
	6	8

Skip counting by

2s	5s	10s
2	5	10
4	10	20
6	15	30
8	20	40
10	25	50
12	30	60

Revision Exercise

1. Complete the following.

☐ + ☐ + ☐ + ☐ = ☐

4 groups of 5 birds make ☐ birds in all.

2. Fill in the blanks:

a. $3 \times 3 =$ ______ times ______

OR ☐ + ☐ + ☐ = ☐

b. $5 \times 8 =$ ______ times ______

OR ☐ + ☐ + ☐ + ☐ + ☐ = ☐

3. Complete the multiplication patterns.

a.

b.

4. Write the answer in the bubbles.

a. 8×3 ◯

b. 4×4 ◯

c. 6×3 ◯

d. 7×5 ◯

e. 9×4 ◯

f. 10×2 ◯

5. Find the products.

a. $\begin{array}{r} 23 \\ \times \ 3 \\ \hline \\ \hline \end{array}$

b. $\begin{array}{r} 12 \\ \times \ 2 \\ \hline \\ \hline \end{array}$

c. $\begin{array}{r} 42 \\ \times \ 2 \\ \hline \\ \hline \end{array}$

8 Introduction to Division

Prior Knowledge

- Counting large numbers by grouping
- Concept of subtraction
- Concept of multiplication

Learning Objectives

- Division by equal sharing
- Division as repeated subtraction
- Relation between multiplication and division

Let's Get Started

Cross the objects and find the differences. One has been done for you.

5 – 1 = 4

5 – 2 = ☐

5 – 3 = ☐

5 – 4 = ☐

5 – 5 = ☐

EQUAL SHARING

Mala buys 6 doughnuts. She places the same number of doughnuts on 3 plates.

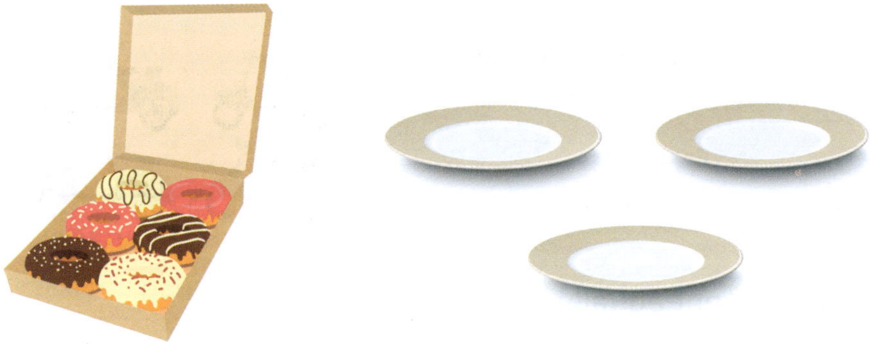

First, she puts 1 doughnut on each plate. Then, she has 3 doughnuts left.

Next, she puts 1 more doughnut in each plate. Now, she has no doughnuts left in the box.

There are 2 doughnuts on each plate.

We have **divided** 6 doughnuts into 3 groups.

We can say that there are 6 doughnuts in 3 groups and 2 doughnuts in each group.

> We write it as: $6 \div 3 = 2$.
>
> $\div$ is read as **divided by**.
>
> It is the symbol for **division**.

Example 1: Share 12 pencils equally among 3 chlidren.

Solution:

There are 4 pencils in each group.

$12 \div 3 = 4$

So, each child gets 4 pencils.

Exercise 8.1

Fill in the blanks by dividing the pictures in equal groups.

1. 2 children share 6 toy scooters equally.

   $6 \div 2 =$ _____

   Each child gets _____ toy scooters.

2. 10 bananas are put equally in 5 baskets.

   $10 \div 5 =$ _____

   Each basket has _____ bananas.

3. 18 fish are put equally in 3 bags of water.

   $18 \div 3 =$ _____

   Each bag has _____ fish.

4. 12 kites are shared equally among 4 girls.

   $12 \div 4 =$ _____

   Each girl gets _____ kites.

5. 10 children share 20 crayons equally.

   $20 \div 10 =$ _____

   Each child gets _____ crayons.

6. 24 books are arranged in a stacks of 4.

   $24 \div 4 =$ _____

   Each stack has _____ books.

DIVISION AS REPEATED SUBTRACTION

Just as multiplication is the process of repeated addition, division is the process of repeated subtraction.

Example 2: 12 balloons are shared among 3 children. How many balloons did each child get?

Solution: Let us divide 12 balloons among 3 children.

$12 - \mathbf{3} = 9$

$9 - \mathbf{3} = 6$

$6 - \mathbf{3} = 3$

$3 - \mathbf{3} = 0$

Subtracted **3** four times.

So, $12 \div 3 = 4$.

EXERCISE 8.2

Solve the following division sums by using the method of repeated subtraction.

1. 9 ÷ 3

   9 − 3 = ____
   ____ − 3 = ____
   ____ − 3 = ____
   9 ÷ 3 = ____

2. 30 ÷ 5

   30 − 5 = ____
   ____ − 5 = ____
   ____ − 5 = ____
   ____ − 5 = ____
   ____ − 5 = ____
   ____ − 5 = ____
   30 ÷ 5 = ____

3. 20 ÷ 10

   20 − 10 = ____
   ____ − 10 = ____
   20 ÷ 10 = ____

4. 15 ÷ 3

   15 − 3 = ____
   ____ − 3 = ____
   ____ − 3 = ____
   ____ − 3 = ____
   ____ − 3 = ____
   15 ÷ 3 = ____

5. 20 ÷ 4

   20 − 4 = ____
   ____ − 4 = ____
   ____ − 4 = ____
   ____ − 4 = ____
   ____ − 4 = ____
   20 ÷ 4 = ____

6. 12 ÷ 2

   12 − 2 = ____
   ____ − 2 = ____
   ____ − 2 = ____
   ____ − 2 = ____
   ____ − 2 = ____
   ____ − 2 = ____
   12 ÷ 2 = ____

RELATION BETWEEN MULTIPLICATION AND DIVISION

10 butterflies can be arranged in groups of 2.

It means **5 × 2 = 10 or 10 ÷ 2 = 5.**

10 butterflies can be arranged in groups of 5.

It means **2 × 5 = 10 or 10 ÷ 5 = 2.**

EXERCISE 8.3

Circle equal groups and fill in the blanks.

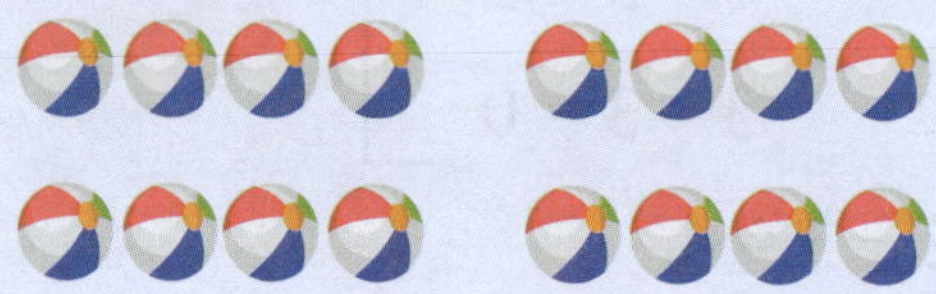

1. 16 ÷ 4 = _____

   4 × 4 = _____

   Each group has ____ balls.

2. 20 ÷ 5 = _____

   4 × 5 = _____

   Each group has ____ ice pops.

3. 28 ÷ 4 = _____

   7 × 4 = _____

   Each group has ____ cupcakes.

KEY CONCEPTS

Introduction to division

- Division by equal sharing
  - 6 ÷ 3 = 2

- Division as repeated subtraction
  - 6 ÷ 3
  - 6 − 3 = 3
  - 3 − 3 = 0
  - So, 6 ÷ 3 = 2
- Relationship between multiplication and division
  - If 2 × 3 = 6
  - Then, 6 ÷ 2 = 3 and 6 ÷ 3 = 2
  - If 5 × 2 = 10
  - Then, 10 ÷ 5 = 2 and 10 ÷ 2 = 5

REVISION EXERCISE

1. Cross out (×) incorrect groups.

a. 

3 groups of flowers

b. 

4 groups of cherries

c. 

6 groups of toffees

2. Divide 18 books into 3 groups. Circle each group.

Books in all = □

Number of groups = □

Books in each group □ ÷ □ = □

3. Divide the following by repeated subtraction.

28 ÷ 7 = □

28 − 7 = □

□ − 7 = □

□ − 7 = □

□ − 7 = □

4. Fill in the boxes.

a. 6 × 5 = □

5 × 6 = □

b. 30 ÷ 5 = □

□ ÷ 6 = □

c. 10 × 8 = □

□ × □ = □

d. □ ÷ 8 = □

80 ÷ □ = □

9 Shapes

Prior Knowledge

- Comparing objects on the basis of size
- Comparing objects on the basis of length
- Comparing objects on the basis of height
- Comparing objects on the basis of whether same or different

Learning Objectives

- Lines
- Flat shapes (2D shapes) and their properties
- Solid shapes (3D shapes)
- Tracing Outlines

Let's Get Started

Observe the different items shown below. Identify the items with similar shape and join them by drawing a line. One has been done for you.

LINES

Shapes are formed using straight lines and curved lines.

is a straight line.  is a curved line.

Straight lines do not bend. Curved lines bend.

FLAT SHAPES

Square 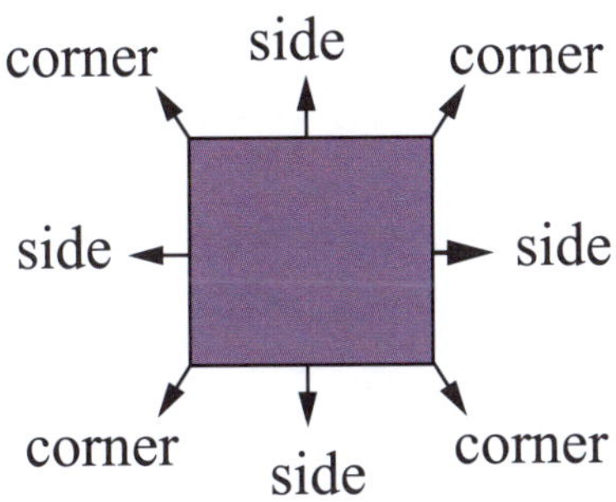	A **square** is made up of 4 equal straight lines. It has 4 sides and 4 corners.
Rectangle 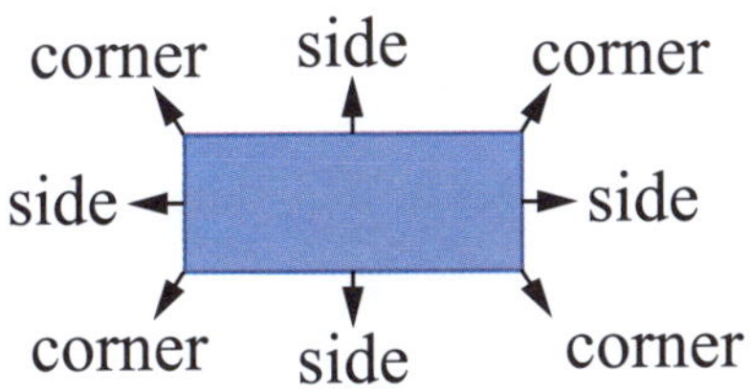	A **rectangle** is made up of 2 pairs of equal straight lines. It has 4 sides and 4 corners.
Triangle 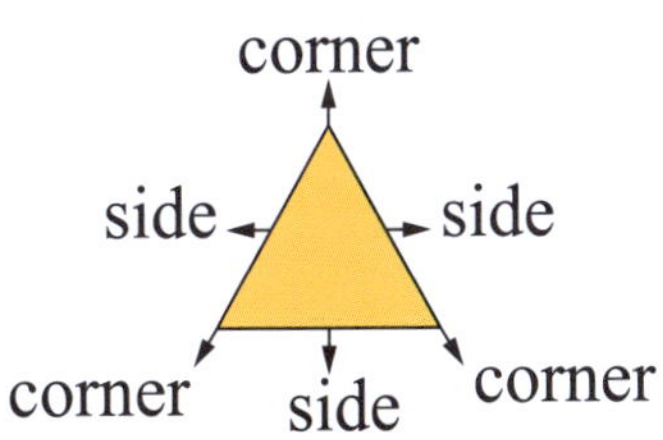	A **triangle** is made up of 3 straight lines. It has 3 sides and 3 corners.
Circle 	A **circle** is round in shape. It has no sides or corners.
Oval 	An **oval** has no sides or corners.

Exercise 9.1

1. Complete the given table.

Shapes	Name of the shape	Number of sides	Number of corners
a. 			
b. 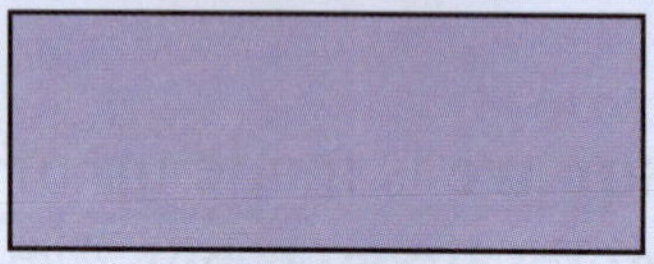			
c. 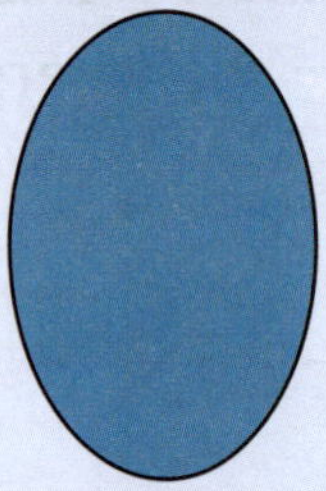			
d. 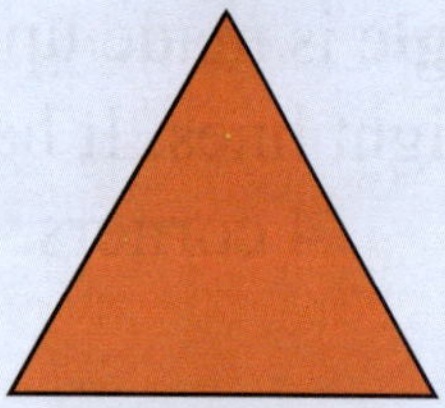			
e. 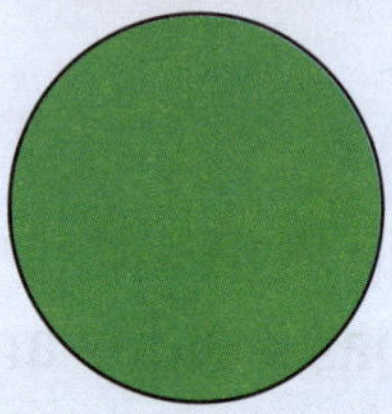			

2. Circle the matching shape.

a. 	  

b. 	
c. 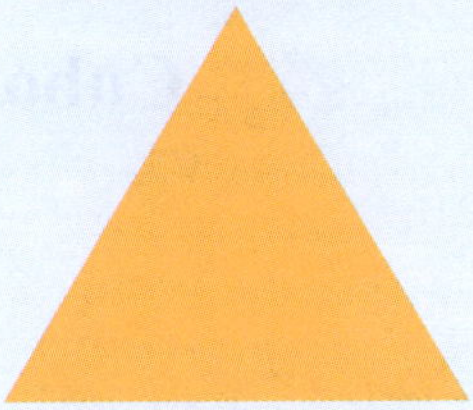	
d. 	
e. 	

SOLID SHAPES

Let us learn about some solid shapes.

CUBE

A **cube** is the shape of a dice. It has 6 square faces.

Cube

CUBOID

A **cuboid** is like a rectangular box. It has 6 rectangular faces.

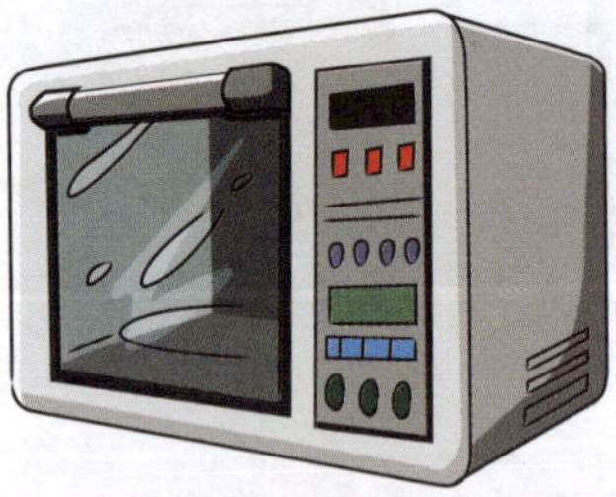

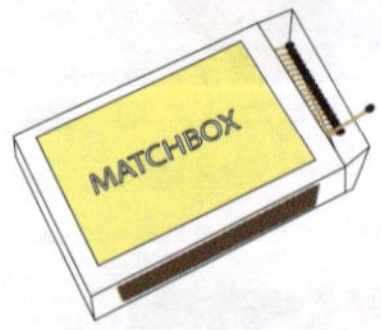

Cuboid

SPHERE

A **sphere** is like the shape of a ball.

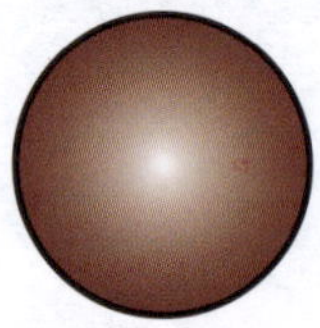

Sphere

CYLINDER

A **cylinder** has a circular face on its top and bottom.

Cylinder

CONE

A **cone** has one triangular face and one circular face.

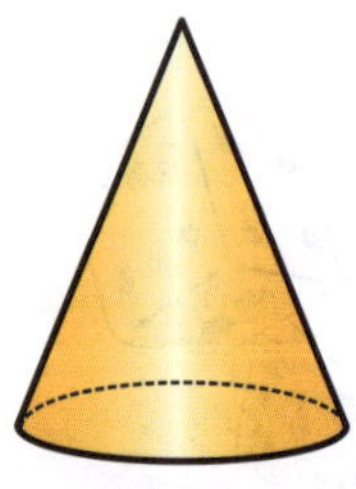

Cone

Activity

Take the following solid shapes, place them on a piece of paper and trace around them. What shape do you get?

Solid Shapes	Flat Shape	Name of the Shape
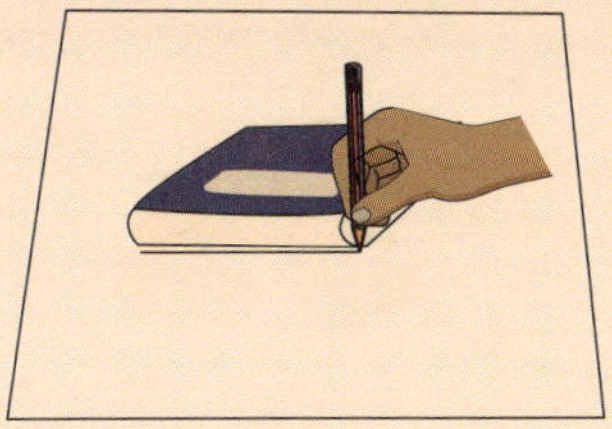		________
		________
		________
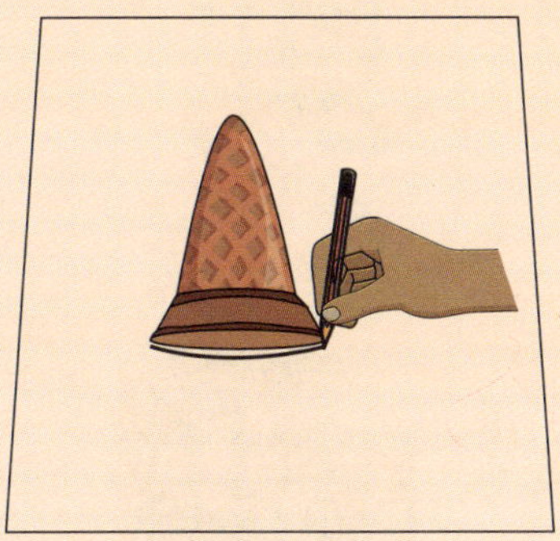	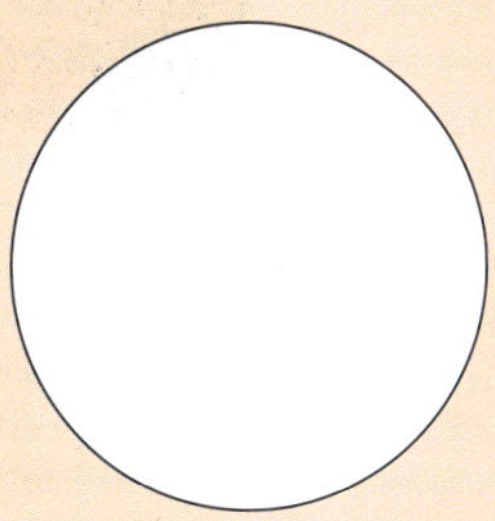	________

Exercise 9.2

1. Tick (✓) the objects as per their name.

a. Cube

i. 
ii. 
iii. 

b. Sphere

i. 
ii. 
iii. 

c. Cone

i. 
ii. 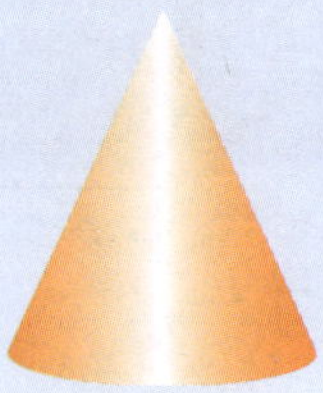
iii. 

d. Cuboid

i. 
ii. 
iii. 

e. Cylinder

i. 
ii. 
iii. 

2. Tick (✓) the correct shape.

a.    

b. 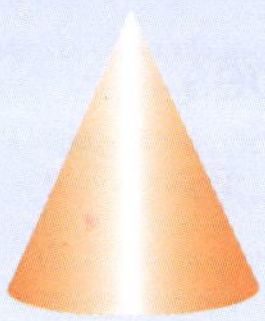   

c.  

d.   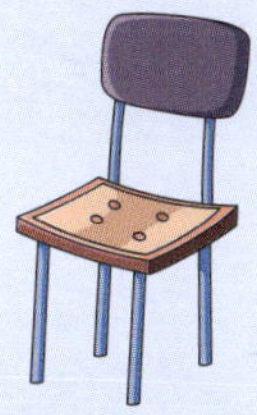 

e.    

3. Use the given words to name the shapes. Also colour each shape.

Cuboid Cone Cylinder Sphere Cube

a. 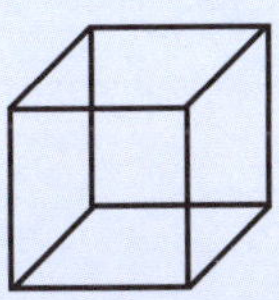

b. 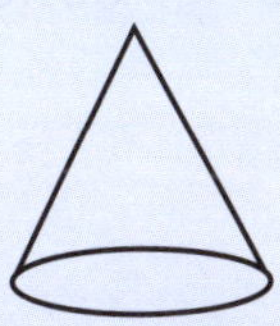

c. 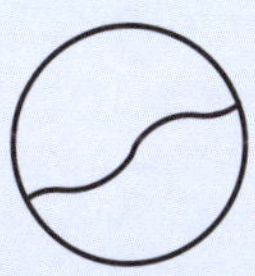

d. 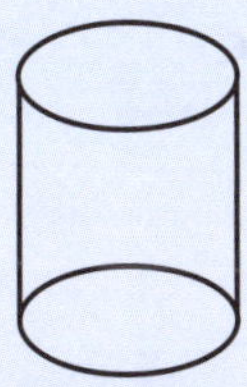

e. 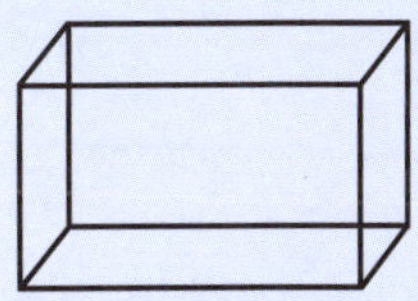

Key Concepts

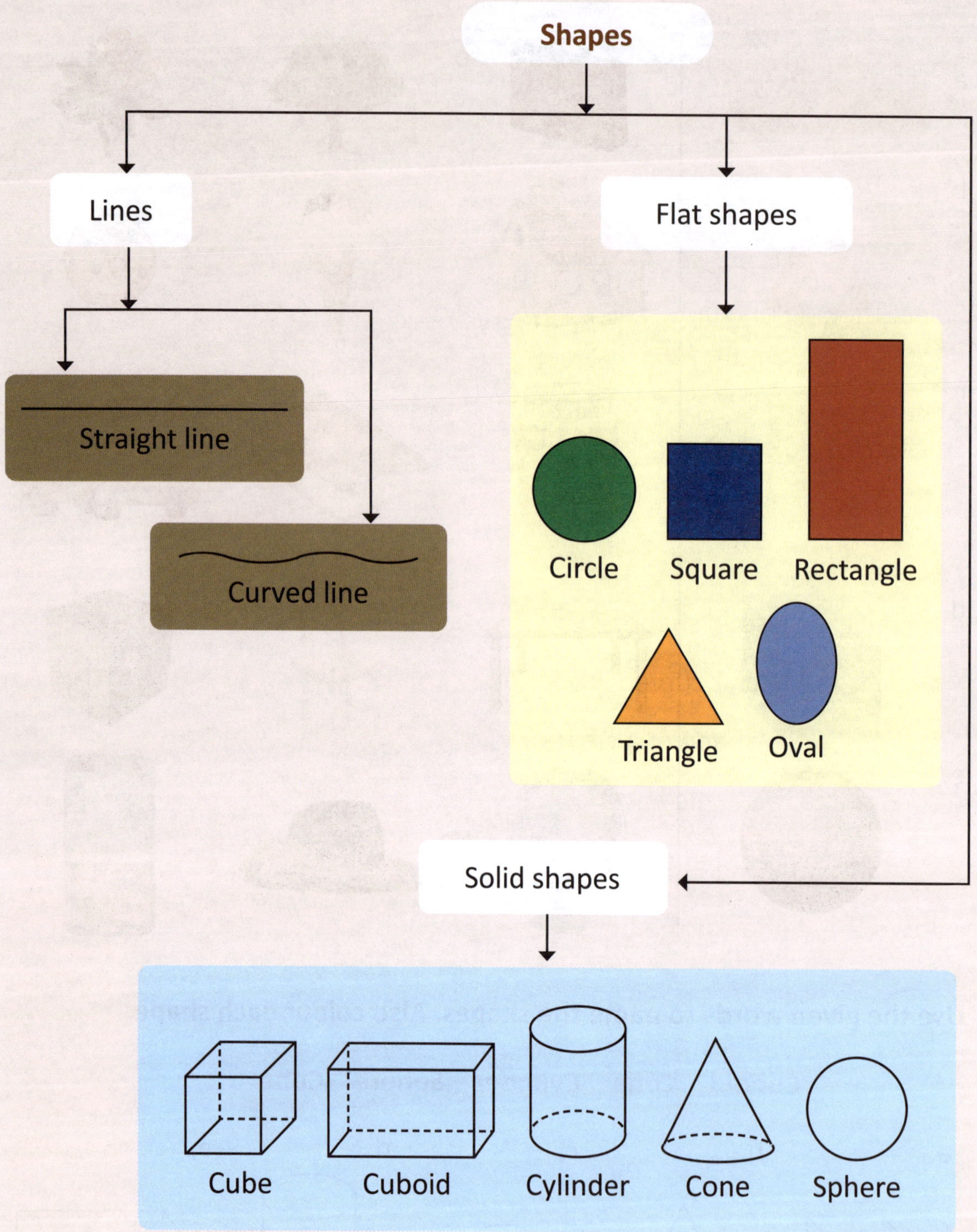

Revision Exercise

1. Choose the correct option.

a. Select the odd one out.

i.  ii.  iii.  iv. 

b. Select the odd one out.

i.  ii.  iii.  iv. 

c. Select the odd one out.

i.  ii.  iii.  iv. 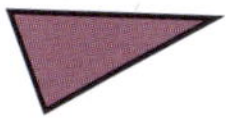

d. Select the odd one out.

i.  ii.  iii.  iv. 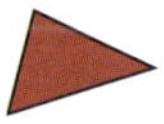

2. Write true or false.

a. A rectangle is a solid shape. ______

b. A circle is made of 1 curved line. ______

c. A globe is in the shape of a circle. ______

d. A square and rectangle have 4 straight lines each. ______

e. A cylinder is a flat shape. ______

3. Write down the names of the flat shapes shown in these pictures.

a. 

____

b. 

____

c. 

____

d. 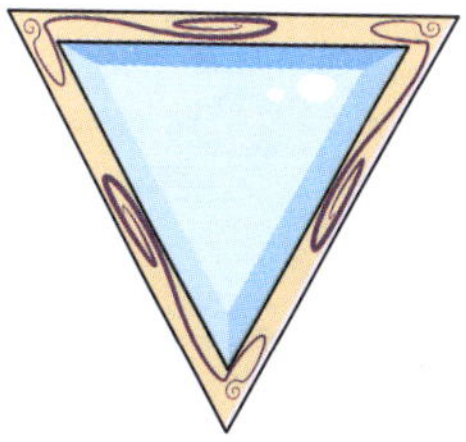

____

4. **Look at the following shapes and answer the questions given below.**

a.	Number of squares	=	☐	b.	Number of cuboids	= ☐
c.	Number of rectangles	=	☐	d.	Number of spheres	= ☐
e.	Number of triangles	=	☐	f.	Number of cylinders	= ☐
g.	Number of circles	=	☐	h.	Number of cones	= ☐
i.	Number of cubes	=	☐	j.	Number of ovals	= ☐

10 Measurement

Prior Knowledge

- Comparing objects on the basis of position
- Comparing objects on the basis of whether same or different.

Learning Objectives

- Arranging the heights and length of objects in order
- Estimating and measuring the objects using non-standard objects
- Comparing mass using the weighing balance
- Arranging the containers according to their volumes and capacities

Let's Get Started

Circle eight differences between the two pictures.

TALL, TALLER, TALLEST AND SHORT, SHORTER SHORTEST

Colour the tall object **brown** and the short object **orange**.

Aarav is taller than Suchi. Supriya is taller than Aarav.

Supriya is the **tallest**.

Aarav is shorter than Supriya. Suchi is shorter than Aarav.

Suchi is the **shortest**.

Aarav **Supriya** **Suchi**

EXERCISE 10.1

1. Fill in the blanks with 'shorter' or 'taller'.

a. The Christmas tree is ____________ than the flower plant.

b. The flower plant is ____________ than the Christmas tree.

2. **Use numbers 1, 2 and 3 to order the objects according to the heights of the trees/plants. Order from the shortest to the tallest.**

HIGH AND LOW

Raj is bouncing the ball **high**.

Ria and Sneha are bouncing the ball **low**.

LONG, LONGER, LONGEST AND SHORT, SHORTER, SHORTEST

Tick (✓) the object that is short. Cross out (×) the object that is long.

a.

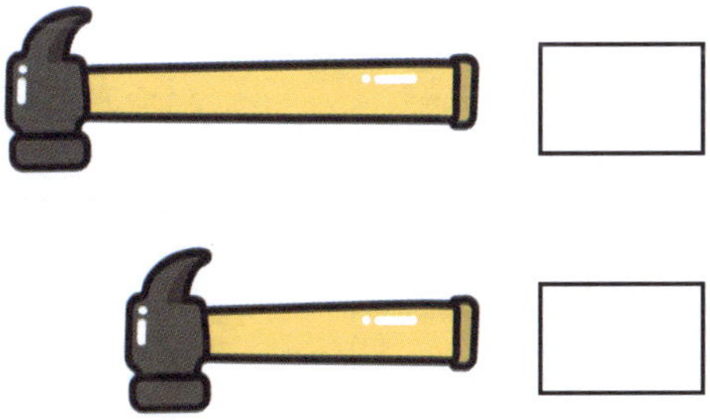

b.

The yellow pencil is **longer** than the blue pencil.

The red pencil is longer than both the blue and yellow pencils.

So, the red pencil is the **longest**.

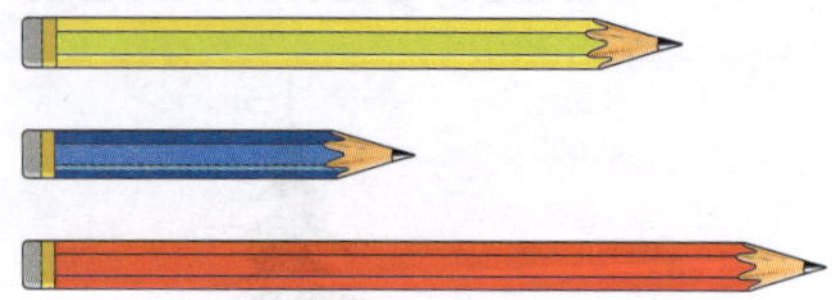

The blue pencil is **shorter** than both the red and yellow pencil.

So, the blue pencil is the **shortest**.

EXERCISE 10.2

1. **Fill in the blanks with 'longer' or 'shorter'.**

   a. The spoon is ____________ than the knife.

   b. The knife is ____________ than the spoon.

   c. The bus is ____________ than the car.

   d. The car is ____________ than the bus.

2. **Fill in the blanks with 'high' or 'low'.**

   a. The blue kite is flying ________.

   b. The pink kite is flying ________.

3. **Use the numbers 1 to 6 to order the objects according to the lengths of the socks. Order them from the shortest to the longest.**

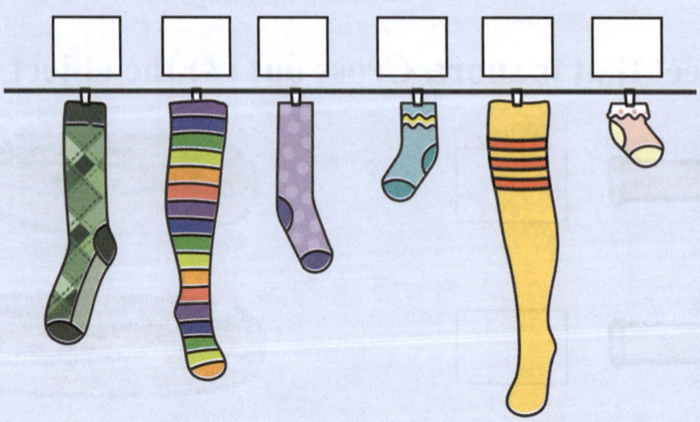

MEASURING LENGTH

Measuring Length Using Body Parts

We often use our body parts to measure the length of the objects.

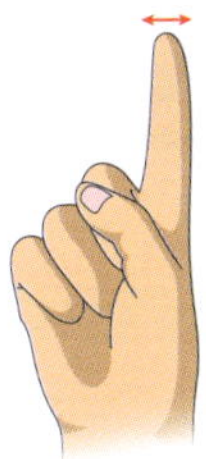

Finger

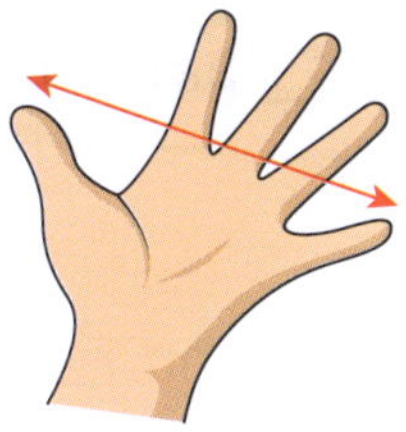

Handspan

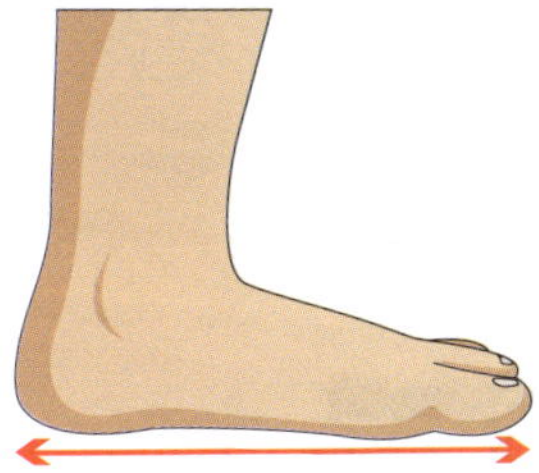

Footspan

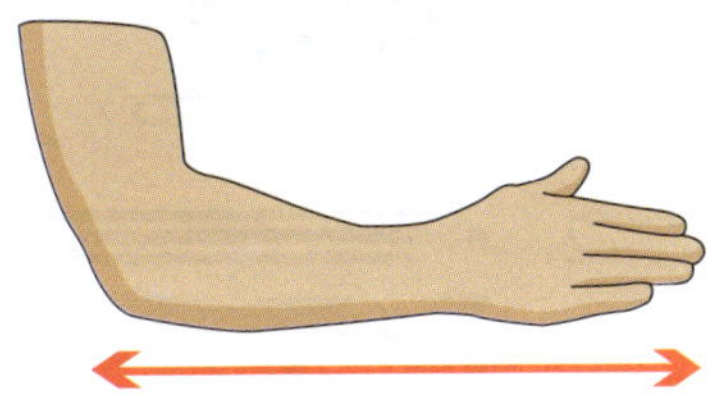

Cubit

Fill in the blanks.

1. The size of my pencil box is about ________________ handspans.
2. The size of my table is about ________________ cubits.
3. The size of my bed is about ________________ footspans.
4. The size of my sharpener is about ________________ fingers.

Look around the room and find the items which measure the following.

a. 3 handspans ________________

b. 4 footspans ________________

c. 2 cubits ________________

Measuring Length Using Non-Standard Objects

We can also measure length using objects such as paper clips, chalks and crayons.

For example, the length of this pen is about 5 paper clips.

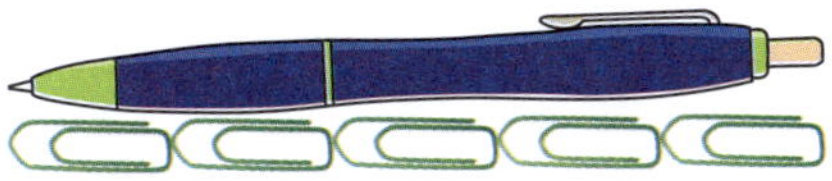

The pencil box is about 7 matchsticks long.

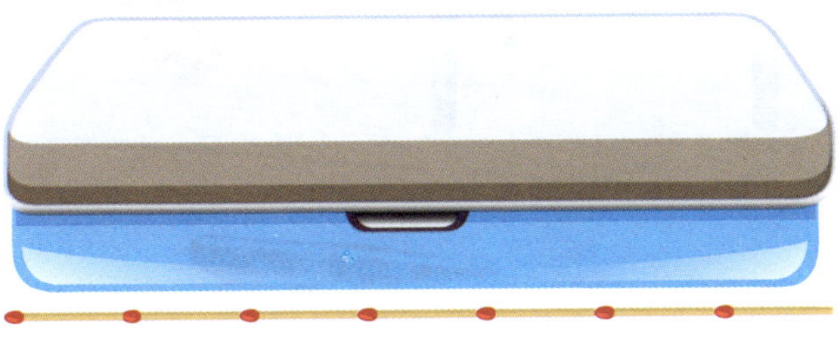

ALERT !

While measuring length using objects like paper clips, we should keep the clips one after the other. There should be no gap or space between them, in a straight line against the object to be measured.

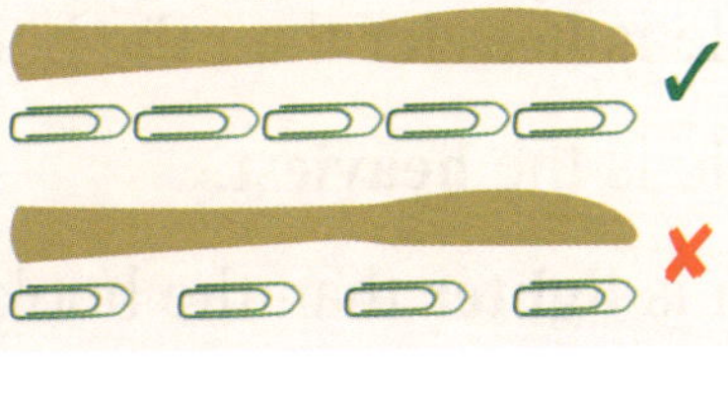

Exercise 10.3

Find the length of the given objects.

1.  = ________ paper clips

2.  = ________ sharpeners

3. 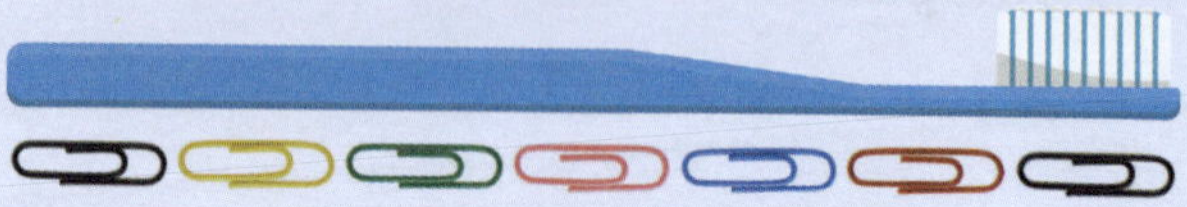 = ________ paper clips

4. 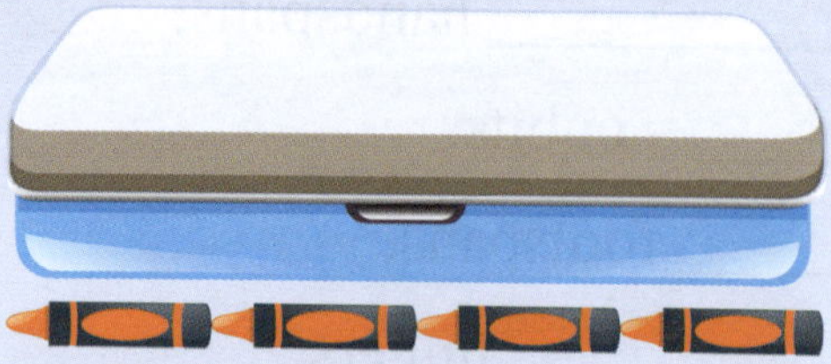 = ________ crayons

5.  = ________ chalks

HEAVY, HEAVIER, HEAVIEST AND LIGHT, LIGHTER, LIGHTEST

Tick (✓) the heavy objects. Cross out (×) the light objects.

a.  ☐  ☐

b.  ☐  ☐

Look at the images given here.

The book is **heavier** than the pen.

The table is heavier than the book.

The table is the **heaviest**.

The pen is **lighter** than the book.

The book is lighter than the table.

The pen is the **lightest**.

MEASURING MASS

By measuring mass, we mean to find out how much an object weighs, that is, how **heavy** or **light** an object is.

We can measure weights by using a weighing scale.

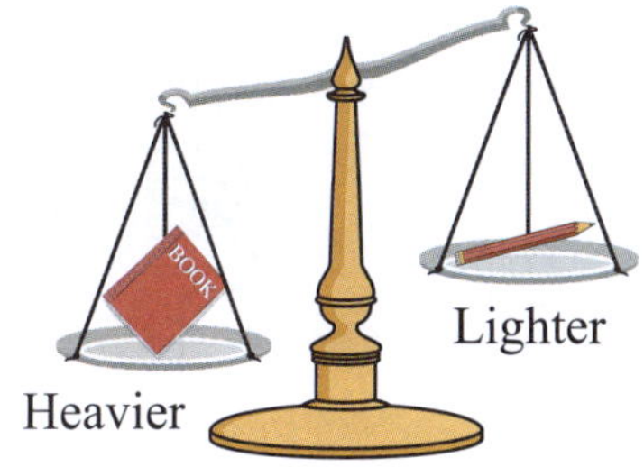

The heavier pan of the scale goes down while the lighter pan goes up.

We can see that the book is heavier than the pencil.

If the weights on both the pans are equal, then the pans balance.

Here, 2 potatoes are balanced or are same on both the sides.

REMEMBER

Bigger objects may not necessarily be heavier than smaller objects.

A lock is heavier than a pencil box.

EXERCISE 10.4

1. In each group, circle the item that is heavier than the other.

a. 

b.  

c.  

d.  

2. Write H for the heavier pan and L for the lighter pan.

a.

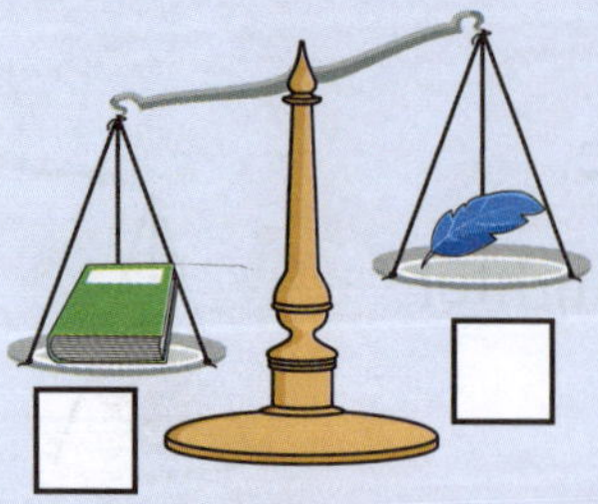

b.

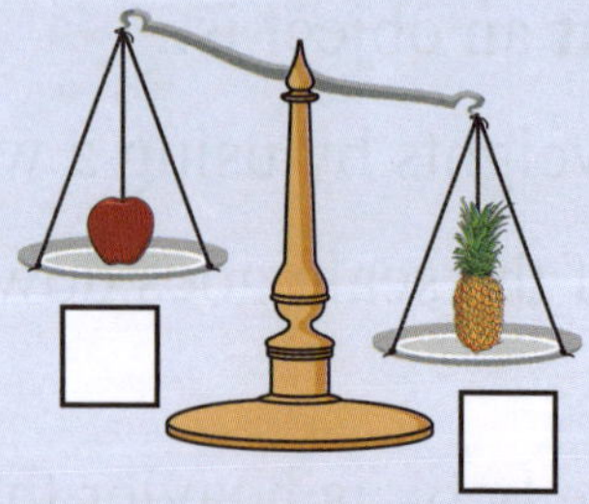

c.

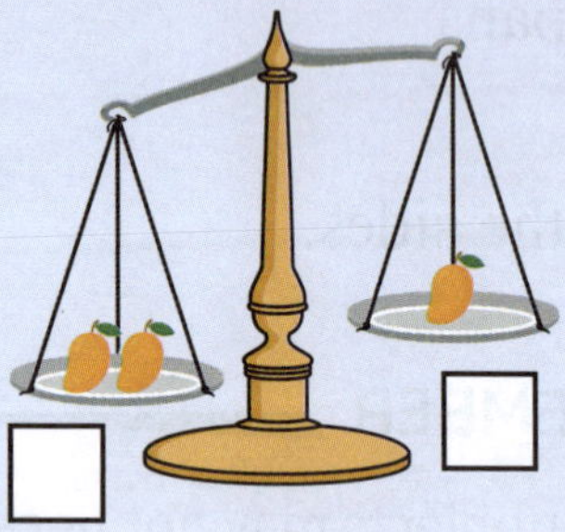

d.

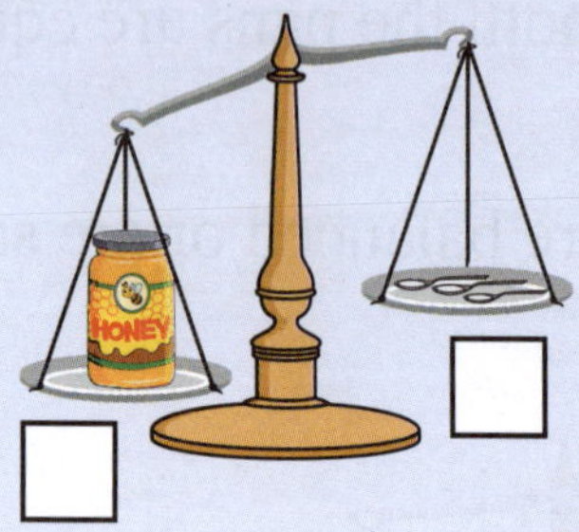

MEASURING CAPACITY

By measuring capacity, we mean to find out the amount of liquid a container can hold.

We use containers such as jug, glass, cup, bucket and bottle to measure the quantity of a liquid.

Cup

Glass

Jug

Bucket

In the pictures shown here, the capacity of a glass is more because it is bigger than the cup. Similarly, the bucket can hold more water than the jug as the bucket is bigger.

Let us pour water from a bottle, a jug and a fish bowl into glasses.

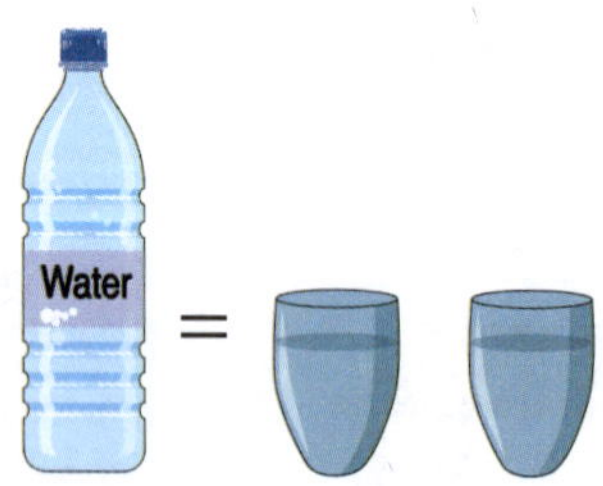

The bottle can hold **2** glasses of water.

Its capacity is **2 glasses**.

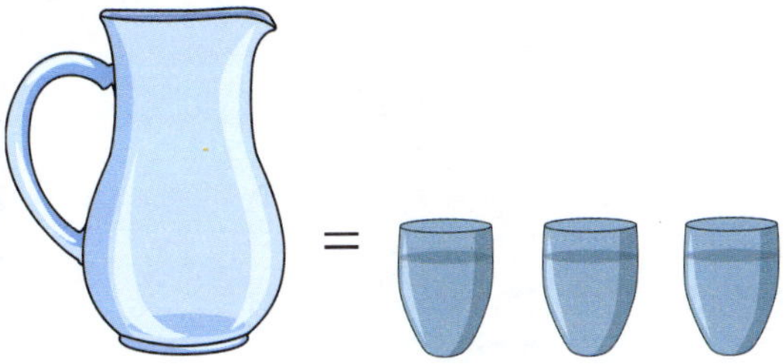

The jug can hold _____ glasses of water.

Its capacity is ______________________.

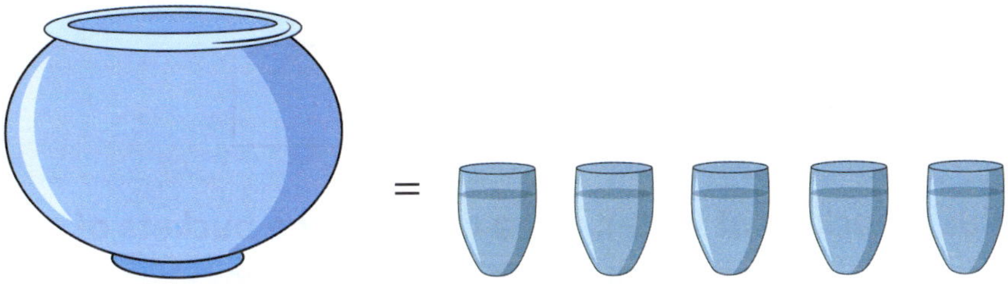

The fish bowl can hold _____ glasses of water.

Its capacity is __________________________.

Thus, the capacity of the fish bowl is _____ (more/less) than the capacity of the jug.

The capacity of the bottle is _____ (more/less) than the capacity of the jug.

Exercise 10.5

1. Write 'M' for the container that can hold the most liquid and 'L' for the one that can hold the least.

a.

b.

2. **A small water tank holds 5 buckets of water. Put a cross on the buckets of water needed to fill the water tanks in each of the following cases.**

a.  = 

b.  = 

c.  = 

Key Concepts

Measurement

Arranging heights and lengths

- Tall
- Taller
- Tallest
- Short
- Shorter
- Shortest
- Long
- Longer
- Longest

Example

Measuring length

- Finger
- Handspan
- Cubit
- Footspan

Comparing mass

- Heavy
- Heavier
- Heaviest
- Light
- Lighter
- Lightest

Comparing capacity

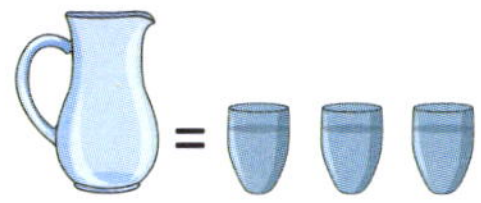

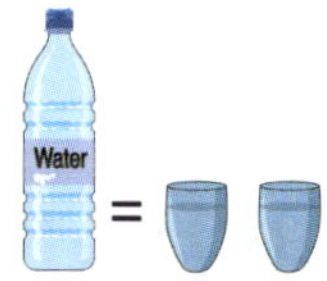

A jug holds 3 glasses of water.
A bottle holds 2 glasses of water.
The jug has more capacity.

Revision Exercise

1. **Tick (✓) the bigger car and cross out (×) the smaller car.**

2. **Tick (✓) the taller boy and cross out (×) the shorter boy.**

3. **Tick (✓) the heavier object and cross out (×) the lighter object.**

4. **Write the length of the given objects.**

a. The scale is about ___________ chalks long.

b. The paint brush is about ___________ clips long.

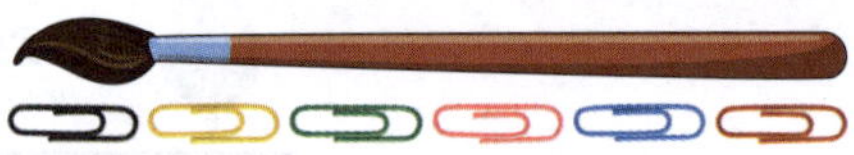

5. **Use the numbers 1, 2 and 3 to order the objects according to the quantity of tea they can hold. Order them from the least to the greatest.**

6. **Which of the two glasses given below has more capacity? Give reasons for your answer.**

a.

Sujit's glass

b.

Anju's glass

11 Time and Money

Prior Knowledge

- Concept of day and night
- Morning
- Afternoon
- Evening
- Night
- Breakfast
- Lunch
- Dinner

Learning Objectives

- Distinguishing between the events that occur at different times
- Long and short durations
- Arranging events happening for shorter/longer span of time
- Days of a week
- Months of a year
- Telling the time by clock
- Identifying notes and coins
- Counting money

Let's Get Started

Tick (✓) the activities that you do during the day and cross out (×) those that you do during the night.

☐

☐

☐

☐

PARTS OF A DAY

Morning

Afternoon

Evening

Night

EARLIER AND LATER

REMEMBER

During the day, we can see the sun shining. During the night, we can see the stars twinkling.

Taking a bath is an **earlier** activity.

Getting ready for school is a **later** activity.

DURATION

Activities or events that take less time to finish are **short-duration** activities. Activities or events that take more time to finish are **long-duration** activities.

Washing face takes **less time.**

Eating breakfast takes **more time**.

EXERCISE 11.1

1. Look at the pictures and fill in the blanks with the correct parts of a day.

I eat lunch in the ____________.

I eat breakfast in the ____________.

I eat dinner at ____________.

2. Write 'E' for the events that happen earlier in the day and 'L' for the events that happen later in the boxes provided.

a.

Brushing teeth ☐

Eating breakfast ☐

b.

Making chapatis ☐

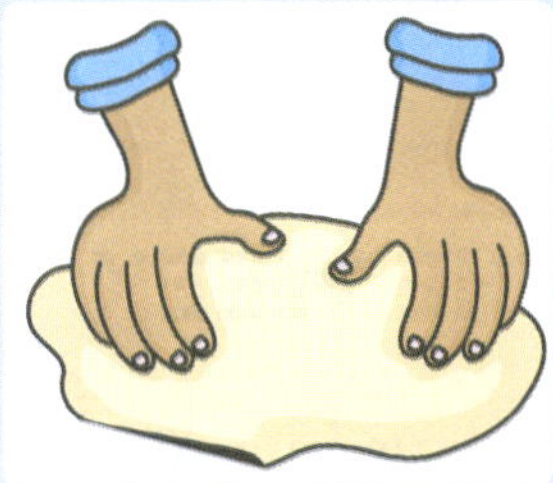

Kneading dough ☐

c.

Doing homework ☐

Sleeping at night ☐

3. **Number these pictures in the correct order that they happen.**

4. **Tick (✓) the activities that take more time and cross out (×) the ones that take less time.**

a. Going to school by car ☐ Going to school on bicycle ☐

b. Watching a movie ☐ Listening to a song ☐

c. Drinking a glass of water ☐ Watering plants ☐

d. Baking a cake ☐ Cutting a cake ☐

DAYS OF THE WEEK

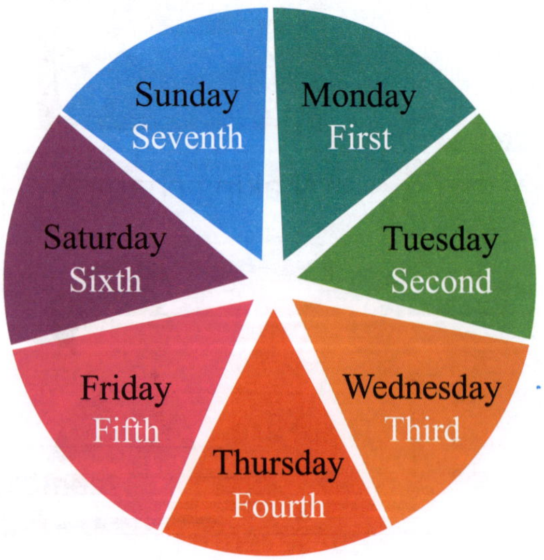

There are seven days in a week.

Monday is the first day of the week.

Sunday is the last day of the week.

Look at the give picture and answer:

- Which is the second day of the week?
  ____
- Which day comes just after Tuesday?
  ____
- Which day comes just before Saturday? ________________
- Which is the sixth day of the week? ________________

MONTHS OF A YEAR

There are 12 months in a year. A year has 365 days.

January	February	March	April
May	June	July	August
September	October	November	December

REMEMBER

- January, March, May, July, August, October and December have 31 days.
- April, June, September and November have 30 days.
- February has 28 days. Every four years, there are 29 days in February.

January is the first month of the year.

December is the last month of the year.

The sixth month of the year is ______________.

August is the ______________ month of the year.

EXERCISE 11.2

1. Write the number of days in each month of a year.

Month	January	February	March	April	May	June
Number of days						

Month	July	August	September	October	November	December
Number of days						

2. Fill in the blanks.

a. ______________ comes between Thursday and Saturday.

b. There are ______________ days in a week.

c. ______________ comes before August.

d. The seventh month of the year is ______________.

e. ______________ is the fourth day of the week.

f. ______________ comes after November.

TELLING THE TIME BY THE CLOCK

There are 2 hands on a clock.

The short hand is the **hour hand**.

The long hand is the **minute hand**.

When the minute hand is at 12, we say **o'clock**.

In this clock, the hour hand is at 2. The minute hand is at 12.

It is **2 o'clock**.

EXERCISE 11.3

1. What time is it?

a.  o'clock

b.  o'clock

c. 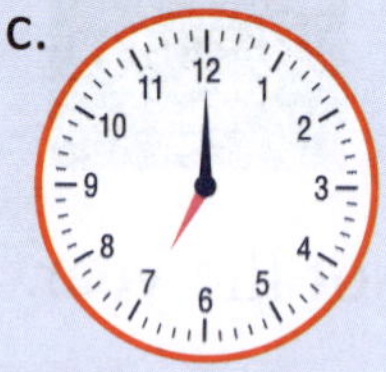 o'clock

d.  o'clock

e.  o'clock

f.  o'clock

g.  o'clock

h.  o'clock

2. Draw the hands on each clock to show the given time.

a.  2:00

b.  11:00

c.  6:00

d.  8:00

e.  5:00

f. 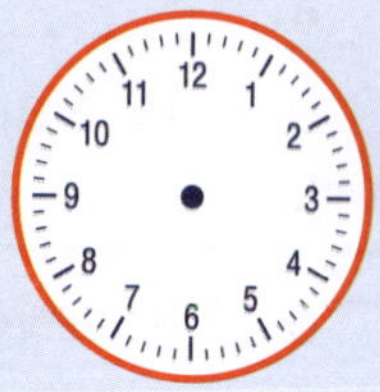 1:00

MONEY

We need money to buy things. Rupees (₹) and paise (p) are the units of money used in our country. Rupees are found in the form of both notes and coins, whereas paise are found only in the form of coins.

Here are the notes and coins that we use daily.

REMEMBER

- 1 rupee, 2 rupees, 5 rupees and 10 rupees are available in notes as well as coins.
- To denote the rupee, we use a symbol ₹.
- Paise is written as **p**.

Notes

1 rupee or ₹1

2 rupees or ₹2

5 rupees or ₹5

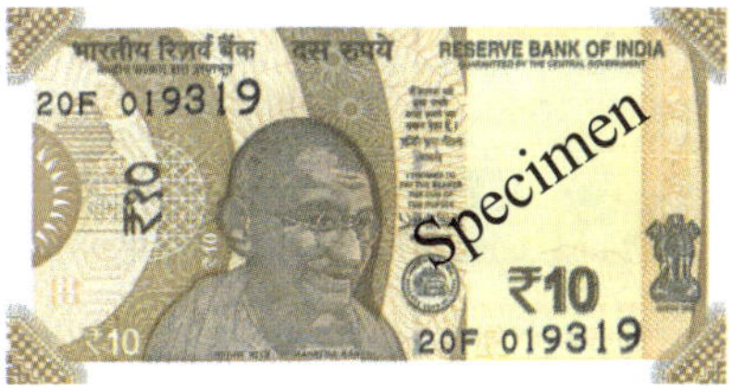

10 rupees or ₹10

20 rupees or ₹20

50 rupees or ₹50

100 rupees or ₹100

200 rupees or ₹200

500 rupees or ₹500

Coins

50 paise or 50p

1 rupee or ₹1

2 rupees or ₹2

5 rupees or ₹5

10 rupees or ₹10

EXERCISE 11.4

Identify the notes or coins and write down the value of each.

1. 

____

2. 

____

3. 

____

4. 

____

5. 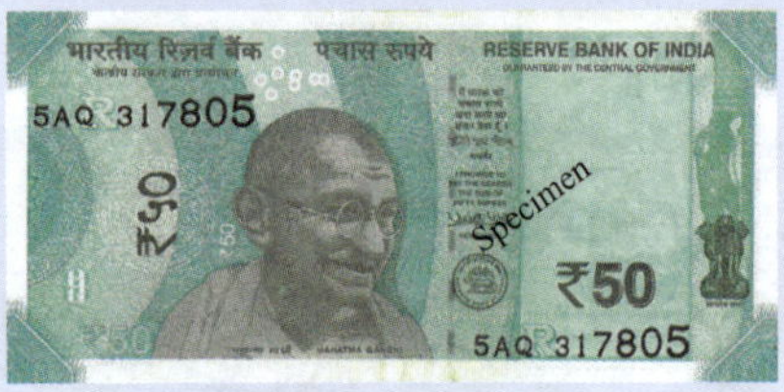

____

6. 

____

COUNTING MONEY

+

+

₹20 + ₹10 + ₹5 = ₹35

+

+

+

₹50 + ₹20 + ₹5 + ₹2 = ₹77

EXERCISE 11.5

Write the amount of money in the price tag.

SHOPPING

Riya and her friends go to the shop and buy these food items.

Look at the items given below and solve the sums. One has been done for you.

 ₹20  ₹15  ₹30  ₹10  ₹40  ₹25

a. 

= ₹60

$$\begin{array}{r} ₹ \\ 40 \\ +\ 20 \\ \hline 60 \\ \hline \end{array}$$

b. 

= ☐

$$\begin{array}{r} ₹ \\ 25 \\ +\ 10 \\ \hline \\ \hline \end{array}$$

c. 

= ☐

$$\begin{array}{r} ₹ \\ 30 \\ +\ 30 \\ \hline \\ \hline \end{array}$$

d. 

= ☐

$$\begin{array}{r} ₹ \\ 20 \\ +\ 15 \\ \hline \\ \hline \end{array}$$

Key Concepts

Time

- **Part of a day**
  - Morning
  - Afternoon
  - Evening
  - Night
  - **Duration**
    - Short
    - Long
  - **Sequencing of events**
    - Earlier
    - Later
- **Days of a week**
  - MONDAY, TUESDAY, WEDNESDAY, THURSDAY, FRIDAY, SATURDAY, SUNDAY
- **Telling time by clock**

- **Months of year**
  - JANUARY, FEBRUARY, MARCH, APRIL, MAY, JUNE, JULY, AUGUST, SEPTEMBER, OCTOBER, NOVEMBER, DECEMBER

Money

- **Identifying money**

- **Counting money**

2 → 4 → 6 → 8 → 10 → ₹10

Revision Exercise

1. Fill in the blanks using correct words.

a. The duration of a day or night is measured in ____________________ (time/money).

b. When the sun rises, we call it ____________________ (morning/evening).

c. I finish my homework ____________________ (earlier/later) than going to bed at night.

d. Solving a sum takes a ____________________ (longer/shorter) duration of time than taking an exam.

2. Write the missing months.

a. March, ______________, ______________, June

b. September, ______________, November, ______________

3. It is time for Sapna's swimming class.

What time is it? ______

4. Count the money and find out the cost of the doll.

5. Number the activities in the correct sequence.

☐ ☐ ☐ ☐

12 Introduction to Data Handling

Prior Knowledge

- Identify objects
- Count till 99

Learning Objectives

- Collecting and recording simple information
- Interpreting the given information

Let's Get Started

Colour by shape.

COLLECTION OF DATA

Data is a collection of information that has numbers. We count the number of objects. It helps us to know how many of each object do we have.

Example 1: Manav saves his pocket money in a money bank.

Following are the collection of different coins he has put in his money bank.

Solution: The given data is about the different coins collected by Manav. Following is the list of each type of coins collected by him.

 7

 4

 3

 2

 are the most in number.

 are the fewest in number.

There is 1 more  than .

There are 5 fewer  than .

There are 7 + 4 + 3 + 2 = 16 coins in total.

If Manav puts 4 more one-rupee coins in his money bank, then how many coins will he have in total? ☐

Exercise 12.1

Look at the number of ribbons Mala has.

1. Count and write the number of ribbons in the given table.

Colour	Number of each ribbon
Pink	
Yellow	
Blue	

2. Which colour ribbons are equal in number? __________
3. What is the total number of ribbons? __________
4. Which colour ribbon is the least in number? __________
5. How many blue ribbons are more than yellow ribbons? __________

Key Concepts

Data handling → Collect and count data → Organize data in table

Collect and count data ↓

There are 5 red butterflies.
There are 3 blue butterflies.
There are 4 yellow butterflies.

Organize data in table ↓

	5
	3
	4

REVISION EXERCISE

Look at the following vegetables available in a market.

1. Complete the given table.

Vegetables	 Tomato	 Capsicum	 Cauliflower	 Broccoli	 Carrot	 Turnip
Number of vegetables						

Answer the given questions based upon the information you collected in the above table.

2. Which vegetable is the most in number? ☐

3. Which vegetable is the least in number? ☐

4. How many carrots are there? ☐

5. Which two vegetables are same in number? ☐

6. Find the total number of vegetables with the vegetable vendor. ☐

13 Patterns

Prior Knowledge

- Identifying objects in different forms and colours

Learning Objectives

- Observing patterns
- Extending and creating patterns of shapes, objects and numbers

Let's Get Started

Draw lines to join the given pictures with their body design.

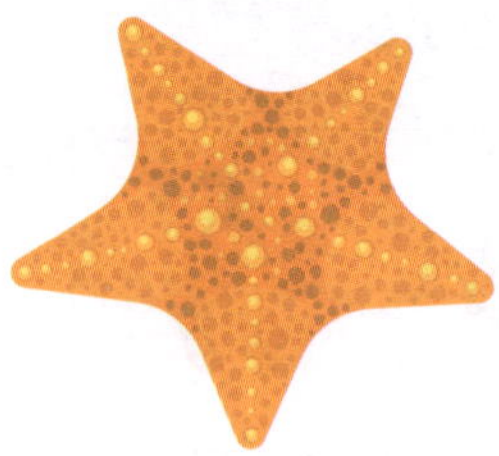

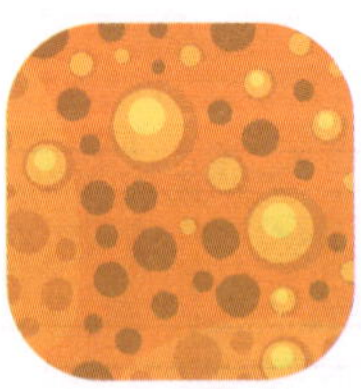

PATTERNS IN SHAPES AND OBJECTS

Observe the following patterns with shapes.

Example 1: Complete the following pattern by colouring.

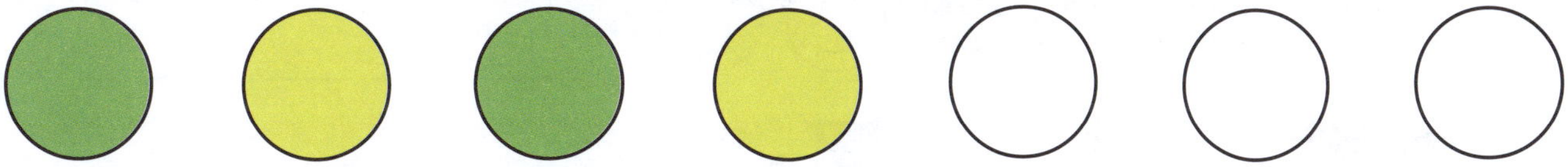

Solution: Here the yellow circle follows the green circle. So, the answer will be:

Example 2: Draw the next two shapes in the given pattern.

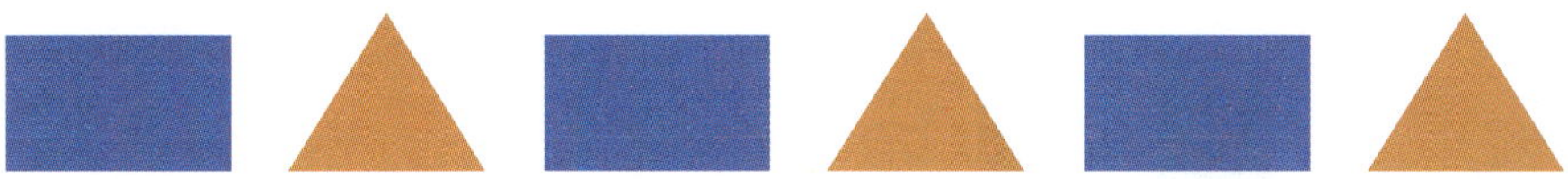 ________, ________

Solution: Here the triangle follows the rectangle. So, the answer will be:

Example 3: Look at the pattern and fill in the blanks.

 ________, ________, ________

Solution: In the given pattern,  ,  and  are being repeated every time.

So, the answer will be:

Exercise 13.1

1. Draw the missing shapes to complete the pattern.

a.  ______, ______, ______

b.  ______, ______, ______

c.  ______, ______, ______

d. 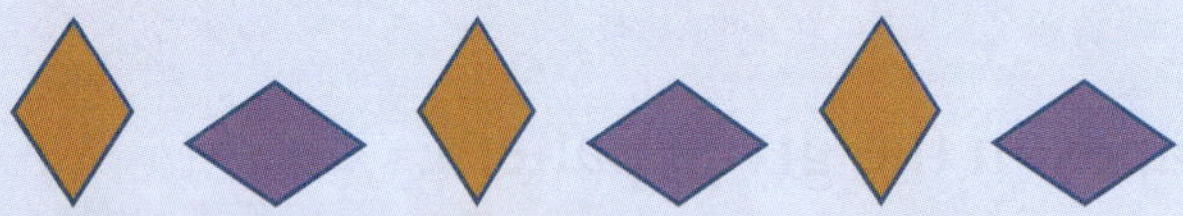 ______, ______, ______

e. 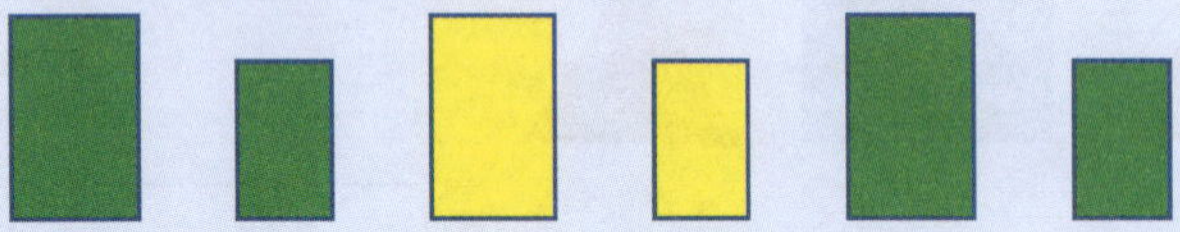 ______, ______, ______

2. Circle the objects that will come next in the patterns. One has been done for you.

a. 

b. 

c. 

d. 

e. 

PATTERNS IN NUMBERS AND LETTERS

A pattern can also be created using numbers and letters.

Example 4: What will be the next numbers in this pattern?

Solution: In this pattern, every next number is increasing by 2. So, the answer will be 10 (8 + 2), 12 (10 + 2) and 14 (12 + 2).

Example 5: Write the next three numbers in the following pattern.

Solution: In this pattern, every next number is decreasing by 4. So, the answer will be 12 (16 – 4), 8 (12 – 4) and 4 (8 – 4).

Example 6: What will be the next two letters in this pattern?

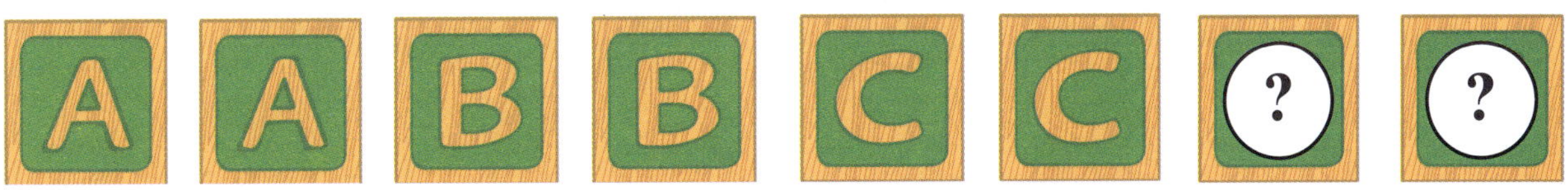

Solution: In this pattern, each letter is written two times. So, the next letter that comes after C will be D.

Therefore, the next two letters in the given pattern will be:

Exercise 13.2

Fill in the missing numbers or letters to continue the pattern.

1. 1, 3, 5, 7, 9, 11, ___, ___, ___
2. 3, 6, 9, 12, 15, 18, ___, ___, ___
3. 8, 9, 10, 8, 9, 10, ___, ___, ___
4. B, D, B, D, B, D, ___, ___, ___
5. T, E, N, T, E, N, ___, ___, ___
6. Z, Y, X, Z, Y, X, ___, ___, ___

Key Concepts

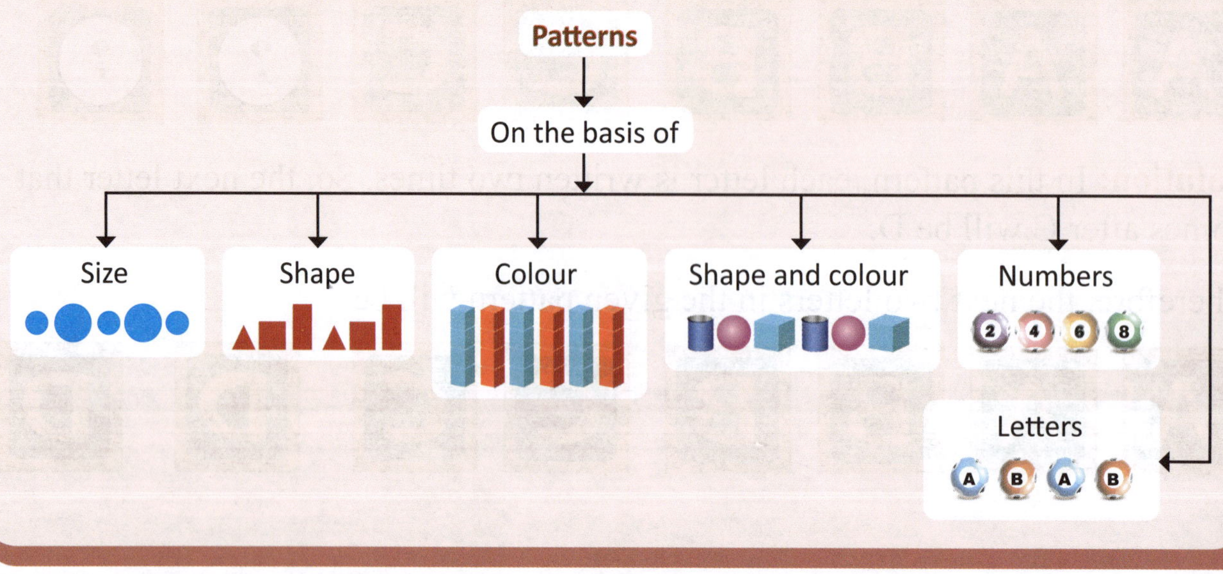

REVISION EXERCISE

1. Circle the shape that will come next in the pattern.

a. 

b. 

c. H E S H E | E S

d. 5 10 15 20 | 30 25

e. 

2. What comes next in the pattern?

a. 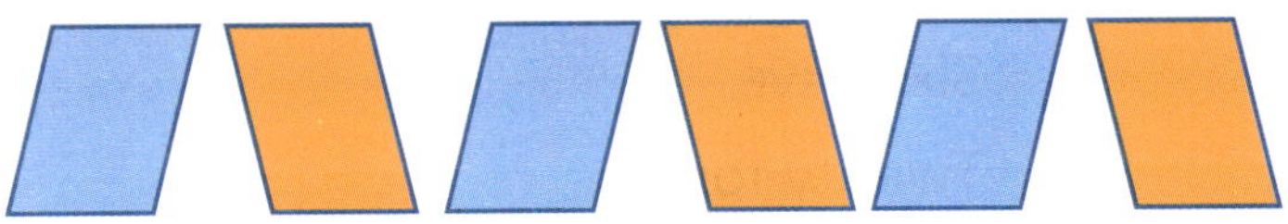 ______ ______ ______

b.  ______ ______ ______

c. 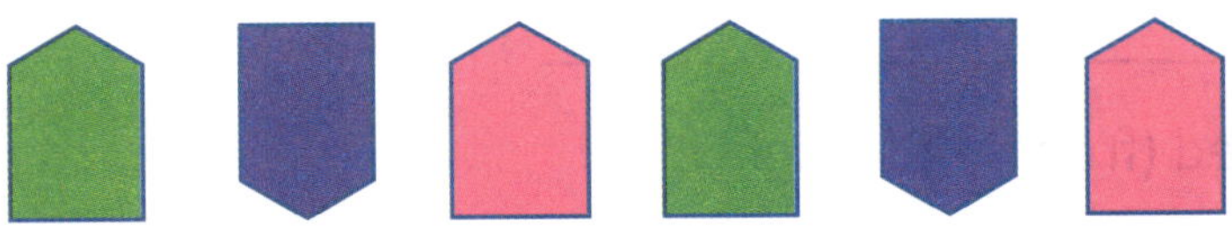 ______ ______ ______

d. 10 20 30 40 ______ ______ ______

e. P Q R P Q ______ ______ ______

Test Paper 1

1. Write the number shown in the abacus.

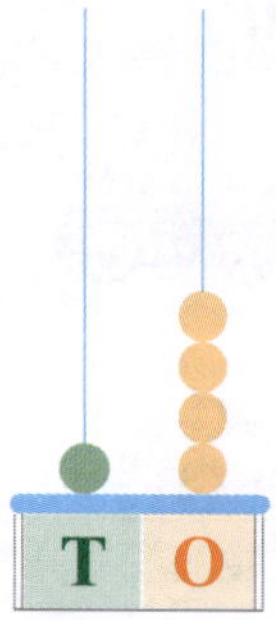

= ☐

2. Circle the biggest and tick the smallest number.

14	8	19	3	1

3. Fill in the blanks.

a. ________ is just before 17. b. ________ is just after 14.

c. ________ is in between 10 and 12.

4. Match the numbers in Column A to their names in Column B.

A	B
9	Eighty-nine
24	Nine
89	Sixty-five
65	Twenty-four

5. Write the following numbers in increasing order.

9	72	29	53	81

________ , ________ , ________ , ________ , ________

6. Colour the ninth flower red (from left to right).

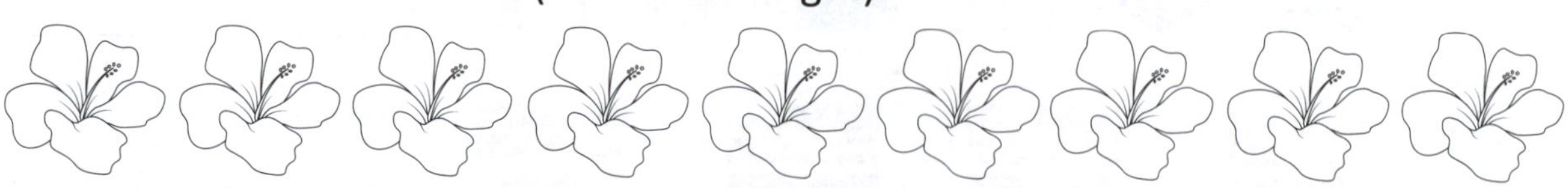

7. Write the place value and the face value of the underlined digits of the numbers given below.

Numbers	Place Value	Face Value
<u>6</u>2	________	________
3<u>7</u>	________	________

8. Solve the following.

a.

	T	O
	1	6
+		1

b.

	T	O
	1	1
+		0

c.

	T	O
	1	9
–		7

d.

	T	O
	1	2
–	1	2

e.

	T	O
	2	5
+	3	4

f.

	T	O
	4	9
+		3

g.

	T	O
	3	3
–		4

h.

	T	O
	7	9
–	2	3

9. Solve the following on the number line.

a. 8 + 6 + 5 = ____________

0 1 2 3 4 5 6 7 8 9 10 11 12 13 14 15 16 17 18 19 20

b. 12 + 3 = ____________

0 1 2 3 4 5 6 7 8 9 10 11 12 13 14 15 16 17 18 19 20

c. 20 – 8 = _________

0 1 2 3 4 5 6 7 8 9 10 11 12 13 14 15 16 17 18 19 20

10. Rajiv has 56 marbles. His friend gives him 7 marbles. How many marbles does Rajiv have now?

11. Ruby has 16 pens. She gives 12 pens to her friends. How many pens are left with Ruby?

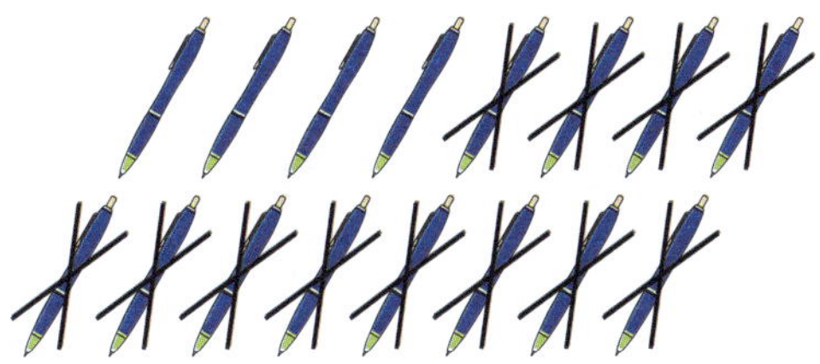

12. Out of 99 students in a school, 37 brought sandwiches for lunch. How many did not bring sandwiches for lunch?

TEST PAPER 2

1. Count with skip counting by 4 on the number line.

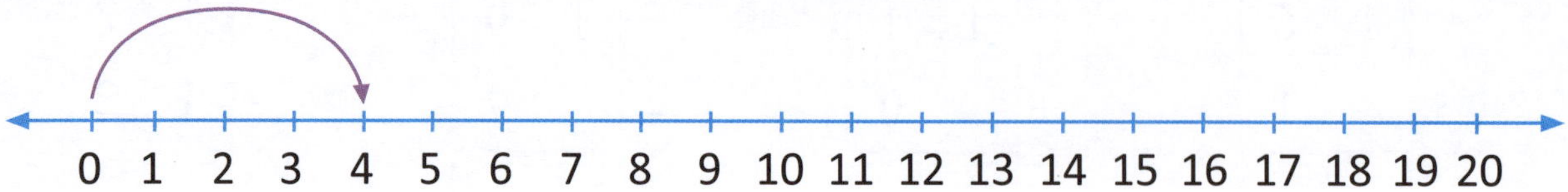

2. Divide 45 balloons equally among 5 children. How many balloons will each child get?

3. Write the missing days.

Tuesday			Friday

4. Match the pictures in row A to the amounts they represent in row B.

A    

B ₹50 ₹2 ₹5 ₹10

5. Fill in the blanks.

a. The ____________ is lighter than the ____________.

b. The ____________ is heavier than the ____________.

c. ____________ is shorter than ____________.

d. ____________ is taller than ____________.

Umbrella

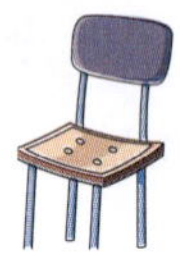
Chair

Mary

Sania

6. Number 1 to 5 in the order these activities happen.

☐	☐	☐	☐	☐

7. Solve mentally.

a. 3 groups of 4 = ____ b. 6 + 6 + 6 + 6 = ________

c. 7 twos = __________ d. 6 × 5 = _____

8. Continue the patterns by filling in the next three blanks.

a. T U B U T U ________ ________ ________

b. 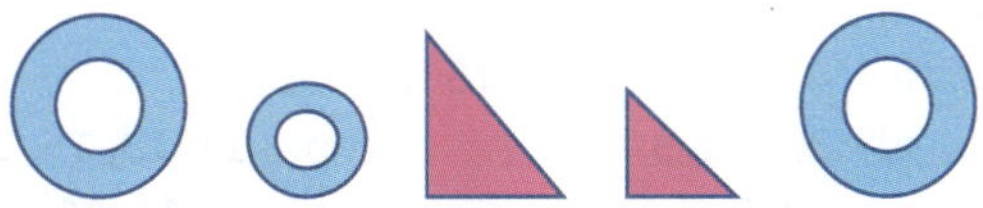 ________ ________ ________

c.  ________ ________ ________

d. M W M W M ________ ________ ________

9. Fill in the blanks with the names of the shapes. Colour the truck using these shapes and colour codes.

 = ______  = ________

 = ______  = ________

10. Pooja has one 10-rupee note and Jack has one 50-rupee note. Who has more money?

11. Draw the hour hands to show the times.

a. 2 o'clock

b. 10 o'clock

12. Look at the picture and answer the following question.

Count the given object and write how many.

Answers

Chapter – 1

Exercise 1.1

1. a. 8, Eight b. 3, Three c. 5, Five d. 10, Ten
2. a. 4 b. 7 c. 5 d. 9
3. a. 0 b. 0

Exercise 1.2

2. b. 11; Eleven

c. 16; Sixteen

d. 14; Fourteen

e. 18; Eighteen

f. 12; Twelve

3. a. 7, 9, 10, 12, 13, 16 b. 10, 12, 13, 15, 17, 19
   c. 4, 6, 8, 9, 11, 13, 14

Exercise 1.3

1. one; two; twelve 2. one; four; fourteen
3. one; five; fifteen 4. one; eight; eighteen

Exercise 1.4

1. 2 2. 6 3. 4 4. 16 5. 12
6. 9 7. 5 8. 16 9. 14 10. 8
11. 18 12. 12 13. 20 14. 10 15. 3
16. 16 17. 12 18. 5

Exercise 1.5

1. a. 14 < 17 b. 15 > 12 c. 11 > 7 d. 12 < 19
   e. 8 = 8
2. a. 3, 5, 6, 9, 11 b. 8, 10, 11, 13, 14, 17
   c. 10, 11, 14, 15, 16, 18
3. a. Greatest: 20, Smallest: 7
   b. Greatest: 18, Smallest: 7
   c. Greatest: 15, Smallest: 10
   d. Greatest: 19, Smallest: 11
   e. Greatest: 18, Smallest: 5
   f. Greatest: 20, Smallest: 13
4. a. 8, 11, 13, 17, 19 b. 12, 13, 14, 16, 20
   c. 12, 13, 15, 18,19 d. 11, 16, 17, 18, 20
5. a. 20, 14, 12, 9, 6 b. 18, 17, 16, 15, 13
   c. 19, 18, 15, 14, 11 d. 20, 17, 16, 12, 11

Exercise 1.6

1. a. Mr. Ahuja b. second c. Ms. Varsha
   d. third e. Mr. Ahuja f. fifth
2. a.

b.

c.

d.

Revision Exercise

1. a. iii b. iii c. ii d. iii
2. a. 12 b. 18 c. 12 d. 15 and 16
   e. 17, 18 and 19
3. a. 13, Thirteen b. 17, Seventeen
4. a. 8 b. 13
5. a. 4 b. 13 c. 15 d. 11
6. a. 3, 6, 8, 9, 19 b. 11, 13, 15, 18, 20
7. a. 13, 9, 7, 5, 2 b. 19, 17, 15, 14, 11
8. a. (18), ~~9~~ b. (20), ~~2~~ c. (20), ~~4~~ d. (19), ~~15~~
9. a. < b. = c. < d. >
10. Fourth position from the left

Chapter – 2

Exercise 2.1

1. 2; 3 2. 3; 7 3. 4; 3 4. 5; 6
5. 1; 6; 5 6. 2; 3; 8

Exercise 2.2

1. a. 3; 20; Twenty-three b. 0; 40; Forty
   c. 9; 60; Sixty-nine d. 7; 80; Eighty-seven
   e. 7; 30; Thirty-seven f. 3; 50; Fifty-three
   g. 2; 70; Seventy-two h. 9; 90; Ninety-nine
2. a. 8; 4 b. 9;7 c. 1; 5 d. 0; 9 e. 8; 2
   f. 5;6 g. 3; 8 h. 2;9
3. a. 82 b. 79 c. 53 d. 41
   e. 67 f. 39
4. a. 2; 3 b. 5; 0 c. 3; 0 d. 4; 5
   e. 7; 1 f. 8; 8

Exercise 2.3

1. a. 5, 6, 7, 8, 9 b. 27, 28, 29, 30, 31
   c. 39, 40, 41, 42, 43 d. 52, 53, 54, 55, 56
   e. 75, 76, 77, 78, 79 f. 82, 83, 84, 85, 86
2. a. 26, 27, 29, 30 b. 35, 34, 33, 31
   c. 49, 50, 52, 53 d. 57, 55, 54, 53
   e. 64, 65, 66, 68 f. 73, 72, 71, 69
   g. 81, 82, 83, 84 h. 91, 90, 89, 88

Exercise 2.4

1. a. 18 b. 27 c. 36 d. 44
   e. 57 f. 62 g. 78 h. 81
   i. 98 j. 90
2. a. 31 b. 18 c. 25 d. 33
   e. 50 f. 56 g. 62 h. 79
   i. 83 j. 99
3. a. 24 b. 37, 38 c. 48, 49, 50
   d. 63, 64, 65, 66 e. 74, 75
   f. 91, 92, 93, 94

Exercise 2.5

1. a. > b. < c. = d. < e. =
   f. > g. = h. < i. >
2. a. 96; 8 b. 81; 5 c. 62; 9 d. 99; 8
   e. 99; 2 f. 85; 29
3. a. 16, 38, 45, 70, 92 b. 15, 41, 58, 79, 90
   c. 28, 30, 47, 61, 99
4. a. 73, 60, 48, 25, 12 b. 80, 62, 41, 35, 19
   c. 90, 64, 53, 27, 12
5. a. Colour the numbers: 75, 76, 77, 78
   b. Colour the numbers: 43, 44, 45, 46, 47, 48

6. a. i. Greatest – 95; Smallest – 59
ii. Greatest – 73; Smallest – 37
b. i. Greatest – 66, Smallest – 11
ii. Greatest – 88, Smallest – 44

Revision Exercise

1. a. iii b. ii c. i d. ii.
2. a. Twenty-one b. Thirty-nine
c. Sixty-three d. Ninety-two
3. a. 1, 6, 16 b. 3, 4, 34
4. a. 5, 6 b. 7, 2 c. 4, 9 d. 2, 3
5. a. 43 b. 56, 57 c. 87, 88 d. 68, 69, 70
6. a. > b. < c. < d. <
e. = f. <
7. a. 51 b. 46 c. 24 d. 18
8. Place value = 60, face value = 6
9. 23, 47, and 39
10. a. 89, 98; 88, 99 b. 24, 42; 22, 44
c. 79, 97; 77, 99 d. 56, 65; 55, 66

Chapter – 3

Exercise 3.1

1. 2 + 3 = 5 2. 1 + 5 = 6 3. 3 + 4 = 7
4. 5 + 2 = 7 5. 6 + 4 = 10

Exercise 3.2

7 + 0 = 7; 6 + 1 = 7; 5 + 2 = 7; 4 + 3 = 7, 3 + 4 = 7;
2 + 5 = 7; 1 + 6 = 7; 0 + 7 = 7

Exercise 3.3

1. a. 2 b. 2 c. 5 d. 4
e. 4 f. 10
2. a. 3 b. 6 c. 9 d. 2
3. a. 3 + 1 = 4

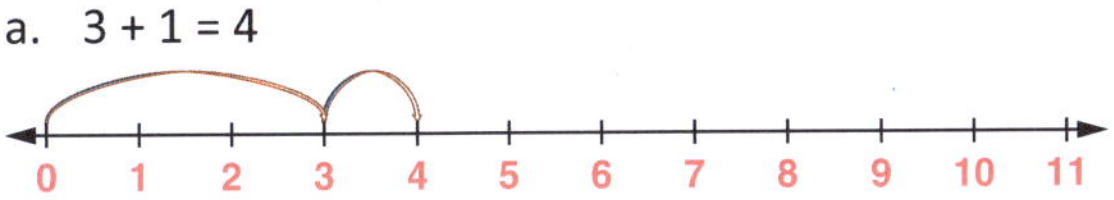

b. 6 + 2 = 8

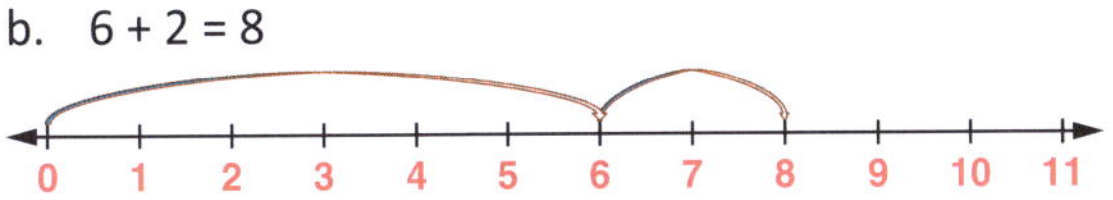

c. 16 + 1 = 17

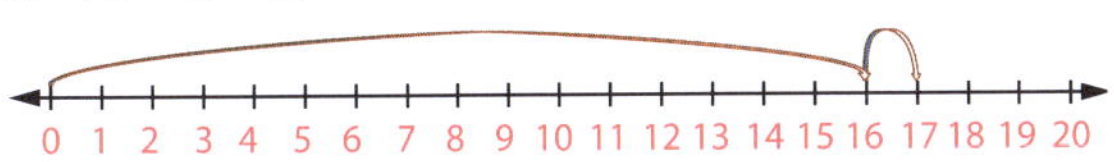

d. 5 + 4 + 2 = 11

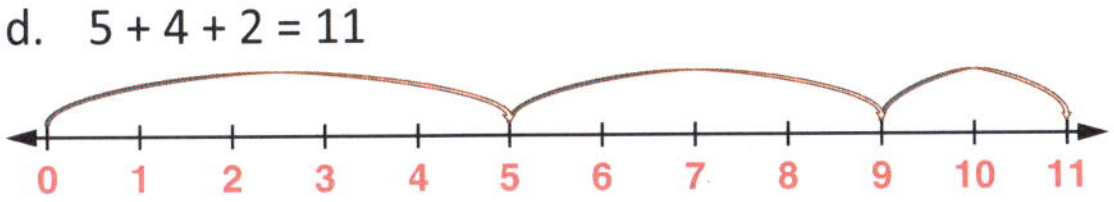

4. a. 6; 6 b. 9; 9 c. 10; 10 d. 12; 12
e. 13; 13 f. 17; 17 g. 15; 15 h. 13; 13
i. 15; 15 j. 18; 18 k. 13; 13 l. 13; 13

Exercise 3.4

1. 15 2. 19 3. 18 4. 15 5. 19
6. 18 7. 19 8. 18 9. 13 10. 19

Exercise 3.5

1. 4 + 3 = 7; 7 2. 4 + 4 = 8; 8 3. 3 + 2 = 5; 5
4.

	T	O
		7
		6
+		3
	1	6

Thus, Sunil has 16 objects in all.

Revision Exercise

1. a. 18 b. 17 c. 8 d. 10
2. a. 7 + 8 = 15

b. 2 + 6 + 3 = 11

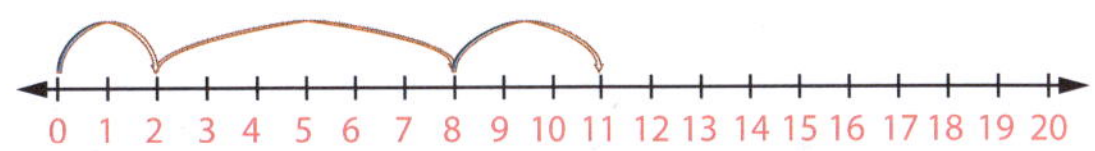

3. 8 + 4 = 12; 12
4. 13 + 6 = 19; 19

Chapter – 4

Exercise 4.1

1. a. 2 b. 2 c. 3 d. 3 e. 3
2. a. 1 b. 2 c. 1 d. 1 e. 4
f. 1 g. 7 h. 7 i. 1
3. a. 1 b. 3 c. 2 d. 1 e. 1
f. 3 g. 4 h. 3 i. 5 j. 8
k. 1 l. 5 m. 1 n. 9 o. 2

Exercise 4.2

1. a. 6 – 2 = 4

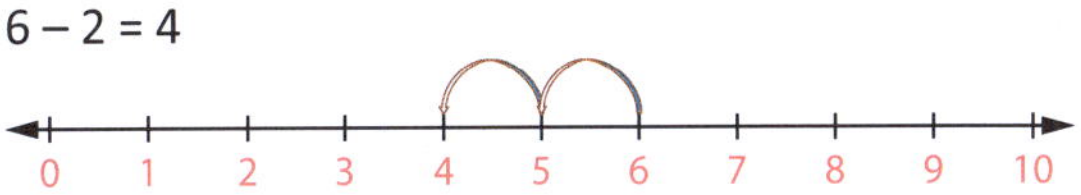

b. 5 – 3 = 2

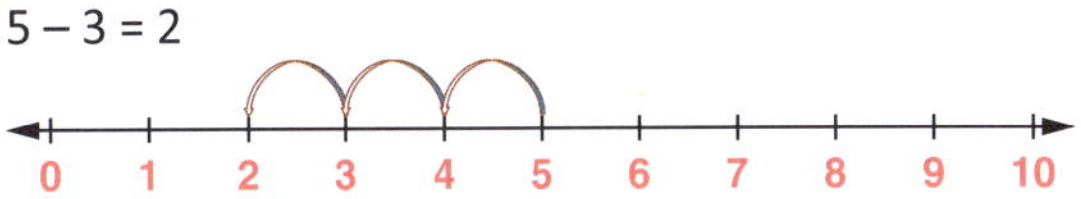

c. 7 – 4 = 3

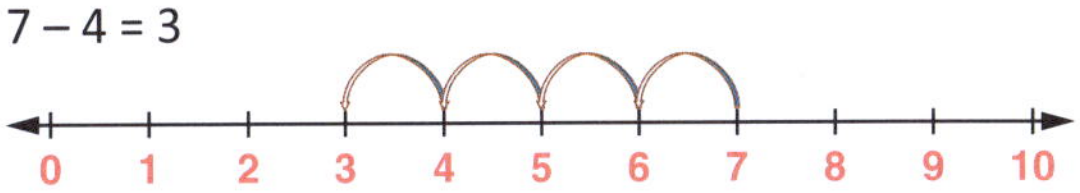

d. 19 – 0 = 19

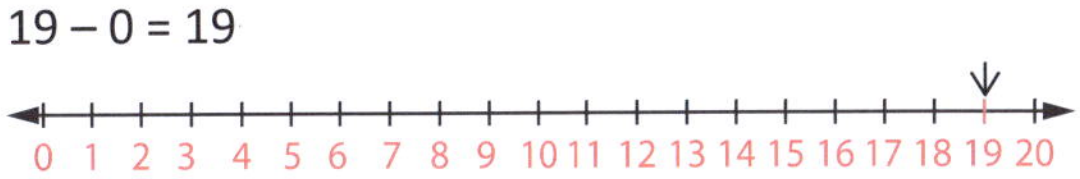

e. 15 – 3 = 12

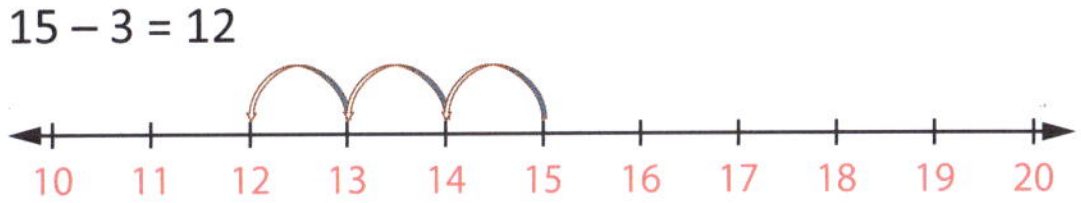

2. a. 11 b. 10 c. 0 d. 15
e. 0 f. 8

Exercise 4.3

1. 5 – 2 = 3; 3 2. 4 – 1 = 3 ;3
3. 8 – 3 = 5; 5 4. 6 – 4 = 2 ;2

Exercise 4.4

1. a. 16 b. 12 c. 10 d. 12
e. 20 f. 12 g. 11 h. 12
i. 11 j. 12 k. 11 l. 13

2.

	T	O
	1	9
–		3
	1	6

16 coins are left with Arhaan.

3.

	T	O
	1	8
–	1	2
	0	6

6 cars are left in the school car park.

4.

	T	O
	2	0
–	1	0
	1	0

10 birds are left now.

Revision Exercise

1. a. iii b. iv c. ii d. iii
2. a. 5 b. 15 c. 6 d. 10
3. a. 7 – 2 = 5

b. 19 – 5 = 14

4.

	T	O
	1	9
–		9
	1	0

Rahim has 10 marbles with him now.

5.

	T	O
	1	5
–		4
	1	1

There are 11 flowers left in Pooja's garden.

6.

	T	O
	1	3
–	1	1
	0	2

There are 2 books left on the shelf.

7.

	T	O
	0	11
	1	1
–		3
	0	8

8 ice cream cones are left.

Chapter – 5

Exercise 5.1

1. 40 2. 60 3. 70 4. 80 5. 52
6. 55 7. 87 8. 68 9. 95 10. 95
11. 68 12. 89

Exercise 5.2

1. 36 2. 88 3. 59 4. 49 5. 18
6. 29 7. 69 8. 39 9. 67 10. 86
11. 76 12. 97

Exercise 5.3

1. 78 2. 97 3. 99 4. 46 5. 65
6. 88 7. 77 8. 45 9. 70 10. 99
11. 98 12. 95

Exercise 5.4

1. 68 2. 99 3. 97 4. 88 5. 98
6. 87 7. 68 8. 69

Exercise 5.5

1. 83 2. 70 3. 52 4. 62 5. 90
6. 52 7. 80 8. 61 9. 81 10. 82
11. 80 12. 92 13. 94 14. 92 15. 91
16. 76 17. 83 18. 93 19. 91 20. 81

Enrichment Zone

1. 377 2. 669 3. 367 4. 579 5. 478
6. 657 7. 649 8. 578 9. 575

Exercise 5.6

1. 12, 6, 18; 18 2. 34, 6, 40; 40
3. 53, 25, 78; 78 4. 12, 14, 11, 37; 37
5. 67, 25, 92; 92 6. 22, 24, 11, 57; 57

Revision Exercise

1. A: 76, 67, 55 C: 43, 60, 568
2. a. 45 b. 47 c. 30 d. 10
   e. 49 f. 40 g. 252 h. 339
3. a. 48 b. 79 4. 26 trees and flowers
5. 79 rupees 6. 43 cookies 7. 89 people

Chapter – 6

Exercise 6.1

1. 30 2. 30 3. 10 4. 40 5. 16
6. 25 7. 18 8. 37

Exercise 6.2

1. 32 2. 44 3. 52 4. 15 5. 22
6. 32 7. 41 8. 61 9. 11 10. 32
11. 70 12. 31

Exercise 6.3

1. 77 2. 70 3. 46 4. 29 5. 39
6. 19 7. 82 8. 35 9. 24 10. 28
11. 8 12. 9 13. 37 14. 37 15. 28
16. 9

Exercise 6.4

1. 57, 7, 50; 50 2. 95, 64, 31; 31 3. 89, 39, 50; 50
4. 55, 24, 31; 31 5. 93, 9, 84; 84

Revision Exercise

1. a. 20 b. 60 c. 15 d. 50
2. A. 51; 48; 25; 13 (Draw a line to match answers from A to B)
3. a. 29 children b. 17 birds
   c. 45 fresh mangoes d. 76 seats

Chapter – 7

Exercise 7.1

1. two; 6 + 6 = 12; 2 groups of 6 = 12
2. four; 3 + 3 + 3 + 3 = 12; 4 groups of 3 = 12
3. three; 7 + 7 + 7 = 21; 3 groups of 7 = 21
4. two; 4 + 4 = 8; 2 groups of 4 = 8
5. five; 2 + 2 + 2 + 2 + 2 = 10; 5 groups of 2 = 10

Exercise 7.2

2. 2 + 2 + 2 + 2 = 8; 4 times 2 = 8; 4 × 2 = 8
3. 3 + 3 + 3 = 9; 3 times 3 = 9; 3 × 3 = 9
4. 6 + 6 = 12; 2 times 6 = 12; 2 × 6 = 12
5. 1 + 1 + 1 + 1 + 1 = 5; 5 times 1 = 5; 5 × 1 = 5

Exercise 7.3

1. a. 12, 12 b. 10, 10 c. 10, 10 d. 2, 2
   e. 9, 9 f. 20, 20 g. 21, 21 h. 36, 36
   i. 6, 6
2. a. 6 b. 12 c. 8 d. 35
   e. 18 f. 16 g. 5 h. 2
   i. 5 j. 4 k. 3 l. 2
3. a. 8 b. 9 c. 8 d. 5
   e. 15 f. 12 g. 20 h. 32

Exercise 7.4

1. 21 × 1 = 21 2. 24 × 2 = 48 3. 33 × 3 = 99
4. 31 × 1 = 31 5. 34 × 2 = 68 6. 42 × 2 = 84

Revision Exercise

1. 5 + 5 + 5 + 5 = 20; 20
2. a. 3 times 3; 3 + 3 + 3 = 9
   b. 5 times 8; 8 + 8 + 8 + 8 + 8 = 40; 40
3. a. 3, 6, 9, 12, 15 b. 10, 20, 30, 40, 50
4. a. 24 b. 16 c. 18 d. 35
   e. 36 f. 20
5. a. 69 b. 24 c. 84

Chapter – 8

Exercise 8.1

1. 3; 3 toy scooters 2. 2; 2 bananas 3. 6; 6 fish
4. 3; 3 kites 5. 2; 2 crayons 6. 6; 6 books

Exercise 8.2

1. $9 - 3 = 6,\ 6 - 3 = 3,\ 3 - 3 = 0,\ 9 \div 3 = 3$
2. $30 - 5 = 25,\ 25 - 5 = 20,\ 20 - 5 = 15,\ 15 - 5 = 10,$ $10 - 5 = 5, 5 - 5 = 0,\ 30 \div 5 = 6$
3. $20 - 10 = 10,\ 10 - 10 = 0,\ 20 \div 10 = 2$
4. $15 - 3 = 12,\ 12 - 3 = 9,\ 9 - 3 = 6,\ 6 - 3 = 3,\ 3 - 3 = 0,$ $15 \div 3 = 5$
5. $20 - 4 = 16,\ 16 - 4 = 12, 12 - 4 = 8, 8 - 4 = 4,\ 4 - 4 = 0,$ $20 \div 4 = 5$
6. $12 - 2 = 10,\ 10 - 2 = 8,\ 8 - 2 = 6,\ 6 - 2 = 4,\ 4 - 2 = 2,$ $2 - 2 = 0, 12 \div 2 = 6$

Exercise 8.3

1. 4, 16, 4 balls
2. 4, 20, 4 ice pops
3. 7, 28, 7 cupcakes

Revision Exercise

1. a and c 2. 18, 3, $18 \div 3 = 6$
3. $28 \div 7 = 4, 28 - 7 = 21, 21 - 7 = 14, 14 - 7 = 7, 7 - 7 = 0$
4. a. 30, 30 b. $30 \div 5 = 6, 30 \div 6 = 5$
   c. 80, $8 \times 10 = 80$ d. $80 \div 8 = 10, 80 \div 10 = 8$

Chapter – 9

Exercise 9.1

1. a. Square, 4, 4 b. Rectangle, 4, 4 c. Oval, 0, 0
   d. Triangle, 3, 3 e. Circle, 0, 0
2. a.  b.  c. 
   d.  e. 

Exercise 9.2

1. a. ii. b. iii. c. ii. d. i. e. ii.
2. a. suitcase b. ice cream cone c. bottle of jam
   d. rubic cube e. globe
3. a. Cube b. Cone c. Sphere
   d. Cylinder e. Cuboid

Revision Exercise

1. a. iv b. iii c. ii d. iv
2. a. False b. True c. False d. True
   e. False
3. a. Rectangle b. Square c. Circle d. Triangle
4. a. 3 b. 2 c. 2 d. 2
   e. 4 f. 2 g. 3 h. 2
   i. 1 j. 2

Chapter – 10

Exercise 10.1

1. a. taller b. shorter 2. 3, 1, 2

Exercise 10.2

1. a. shorter b. longer c. longer d. shorter
2. a. high b. low
3. 4, 5, 3, 2, 6,1

Exercise 10.3

1. a. 3 paper clips b. 5 sharpeners
   c. 7 paper clips d. 4 crayons e. 6 chalks

Exercise 10.4

1. a. Elephant b. Apple c. Table d. Wood
2. a. H, L b. L, H c. H, L d. H, L

Exercise 10.5

1. a.  - M  - L
   b.  - L  - M
2. a.  = 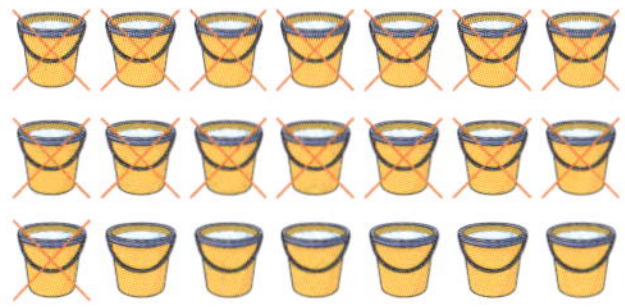
   b.  = 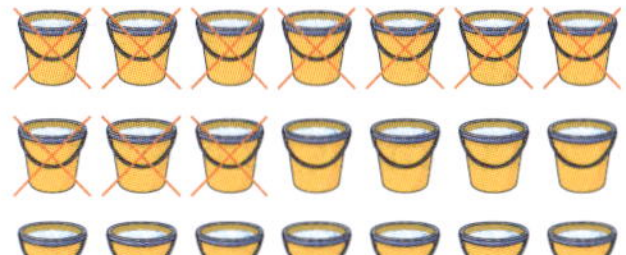
   c.  = 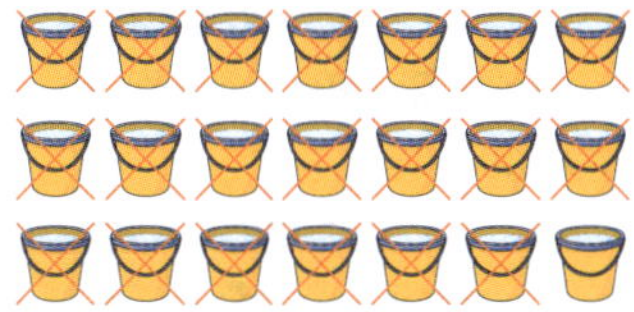

Revision Exercise

1.  - ×  - ✓
2.  - ✓  - × 3.  ×  ✓
4. a. 4 b. 6 5. 2, 3, 1
6. Anju's glass has more capacity than Sujit's glass as it can hold more juice.

Chapter – 11

Exercise 11.1

1. afternoon, morning, night (Pictures from left to right)
2. a. E, L b. L, E c. E, L
3. 4. 3, 1, 2, 5, 6 (pictures from left to right)
4. a. ×, ✓ b. ✓, × c. ×, ✓ d. ✓, ×

Exercise 11.2

1. 31; 28 or 29; 31; 30, 31; 30; 31; 31; 30; 31; 30; 31
2. a. Friday b. 7 c. July
   d. July e. Thursday f. December

Exercise 11.3

1. a. 12 o' clock b. 4 o' clock c. 7 o' clock
   d. 3 o' clock e. 5 o' clock f. 9 o' clock
   g. 11 o' clock h. 10 o' clock

2. a.  b.  c. 

d.  e.  f. 

Exercise 11.4

1. 2-rupee coin 2. 10-rupee coin 3. 10-rupee note
4. 5-rupee note 5. 50-rupee note 6. 20-rupee note

Exercise 11.5

1. ₹15 2. ₹70 3. ₹80 4. ₹72

Revision Exercise

1. a. time b. morning c. earlier d. shorter
2. a. April, May b. October, December
3. 4 o' clock 4. Cost of doll is ₹75.
5. 3, 2, 4, 1 (Pictures from left to right)

Chapter – 12

Exercise 12.1

1. 6, 5, 6 2. Pink and blue 3. 17
4. Yellow 5. 1

Revision Exercise

1.

Vegetables	 Tomato	 Capsicum	 Cauliflower	 Broccoli	 Carrot	 Turnip
Number of vegetables	9	8	3	4	5	2

2. Tomato 3. Turnip 4. 5
5. None of them 6. 31

Chapter – 13

Exercise 13.1

1. a.  b. 
c. 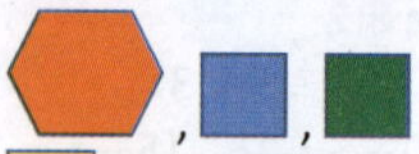 d. 
e. 

2. a.  b.  c.  d. 
e. 

Exercise 13.2

1. 13, 15, 17 2. 21, 24, 27 3. 8, 9, 10
4. B, D, B 5. T, E, N 6. Z, Y, X

Revision Exercise

1. a.  b.  c. 

d. 

e. 

2. a. 
b. 
c. 
d. 

e.